THE KEY
TO THE OTHER

Anna Lewins

THE KEY TO THE OTHER

Blackie

British Library Cataloguing in Publication Data

Lewins, Anna
The key to the other.
I. Title
823'.914[J]   PZ7

ISBN 0-216-92331-X

Blackie and Son Ltd
7 Leicester Place
London WC2H 7BP

Printed in Great Britain by
Thomson Litho Ltd, East Kilbride, Scotland

Contents

Acknowledgement

Many thanks to Dr Margaret Pollak, Medical Director of the Sheldon Children's Centre, London, for her kind assistance and expert advice during the writing of this book. Also, my thanks to the British Dyslexia Association for their fund of useful information and encouragement.

The Key

'The other what?' Flip leapt out of his dad's way. 'The label says, "The Key to the Other. Please do not touch." What do you think?'

'I think you shouldn't touch it.' Mr Sparrow dumped his pile of blankets on the kitchen floor. 'How about helping Bim?'

A mound of towels waddled into the door-frame and said, 'Ouch!' Red curls and freckles emerged, then his sister's black eye-brows.

'Careful, Bim.' Flip unloaded her while their dad disappeared back into the yard. With any luck, they would finish unpacking before tea. It would be their first tea in their new home and Flip's neck goose-pimpled with excitement.

'What's the key for?' Bim prodded the iron with a grubby thumb.

'I don't know.' The key had dangled behind the door on a dirty loop of rope. Flip might have ignored it but its label puzzled him. 'Come on, we'd better help Dad.'

Perched inside the elbow of Caliburn Hill, the Sparrows' new home was a world away from their London flat. For a start, it was a shop at the front and a house at the back. The shop windows over-

7

looked the pavement. To the right, double gates opened into the cobbled yard beside the kitchen.

Everything the Sparrows owned sank into the crust of icing-sugar at the bottom of the van. Her mouth full of icing-dust, Mrs Sparrow wrenched the last suitcase on to the road. A pair of tights floated into the gutter, then a crushed paper hat with 'Bert's Burger Bar' written on it.

'I've just about had enough.' Mrs Sparrow slumped on to the suitcase. 'My back aches and my head aches . . . And I wish we knew what we're letting ourselves in for. We don't know the first thing about selling herbs.'

Mr Sparrow squeezed her shoulder. 'We'll learn quick enough, love. Anyway, it has to be better than Bert's Burger Bar. If I'd stayed there much longer, I'd have been smoked like a kipper.' He picked the paper hat up and spun it around his thumb. 'First thing tomorrow, I'll start baking cakes. Now go on, Bim-Bim. Find the kettle. We could all do with a nice pot of tea.'

Mrs Sparrow looked up. 'And wash those hands!'

Bim slouched around the kitchen, reading the labels. Everything had a label. A button hid in the larder wall and its label said, 'Do not touch this button.' Bim glanced over her shoulder. Flip had his back to her, so she dug the button with her elbow. A small door opened, a spring twanged and Bim vanished in a cloud of flour.

'Bim!' Flip stared at her. 'You're all white!'

The other side of the label said, 'Told you so.'

'You shut up.' Bim stomped past him. 'I don't think it's funny!'

'You can't see yourself.' Flip fell against the sink,

8

giggling. 'Hey, this button says, "For burglars". Look, this red one.'

'Don't touch it!' Bim dragged him away. 'It'll probably flatten you. This place is WEIRD!'

While the kettle boiled, Flip wandered into the hall and on to the stairs. Halfway up he stiffened, decided that he was dreaming but turned around, anyway. On the opposite wall, the big mirror reflected his skinny body and red hair. Above his mirror head, black letters burned 'Philip Sparrow who likes bicycles' into the glass.

'Bim!' Flip yelled. 'Bim, come here! Stand on the stairs.'

Grumbling, Bim marched up the stairs. The letters on the mirror changed to 'Beverley Sparrow with flour in her hair'.

'How can it do that?' Flip ran a finger over the black letters. 'They're under the glass. How can they change, like that?'

Bim sniffed, still sulking about the flour. 'Who cares? Anyway, the kettle's boiling.'

'I just want a quick look upstairs.' Flip grinned at her foggy hair. 'It was right about the flour, anyway.'

Suddenly wanting that cup of tea, Flip jogged along the landing, glanced into each bedroom and hurried back. At the end of the banister rail, a small button said, 'The quick way down.' Already on the top step, sniffing the steam hitting the tea-leaves, Flip pressed the button without thinking. The stairs crashed flat and Flip crashed flat with them, skidding down the steep carpet slide with elbow-skinning speed. Feet in the air, carpet-burns branding his bumpy spine, Flip shot across the hall into the broom cupboard. Brushes pelted his shoulders and a month

9

of dust billowed around him. He crawled out, spluttering.

'Now who's all white?' Bim smirked. 'I told you not to touch the buttons.'

No one had remembered to lock the van, so Flip trotted into the street with the keys. The posters in the hairdressing salon next door told Flip to 'Support the Hospital Fund' and 'Keep Our Town Tidy'. Blinking a lump of fringe out of his eyes, he noticed a car parked on the street corner. The sun glinted on its black paintwork and on its black windows. A man stood beside it and watched Flip.

'Who . . .?' Flip winced as the car scraped burnt rubber onto the tarmac. 'Now that's dangerous!'

Turning away, Flip spotted something in the shop door—a brass eye in the wood. He guessed it was a fancy sort of spyhole. When he squinted into it, another eye squinted back. Then it winked at him.

Mr Sparrow looked up from the kitchen window. 'Come on, Flippy. Let's drink a toast.' He handed Flip a mug of tea. 'To Weston St Brigid and all who sail in her. To the shop and a new start. And God bless Great-grandad Sparrow.'

The letter from Great-grandad Sparrow had arrived seven weeks ago and Flip remembered every word . . .

'I'm off, for a while. Look after the shop and don't mess with the buttons. Everything's labelled and there's a bit of money. I expect you're broke. Sparrows never earn much. Your kids will love the place.'

According to the solicitor, Great-grandad Sparrow had left Weston St Brigid with no forwarding address. He had asked his only relatives, David Sparrow and his family, to run the shop until he returned. There was enough money to manage for one month. After that, the new Sparrows were on their own. And they had to move in before the Weston Great Show.

By the time that Flip's parents had settled everything in London, they had almost run out of time. It was the first week of the school holidays and the Show was next weekend.

'This is quite a place, all right. So far, my favourite's the spyhole,' Mr Sparrow said. 'Did I make you jump, Flippy?'

Flip nodded. 'A bit.'

Another brass eye glittered next to the pantry.

'There's one in the hall, as well.' His dad walked to the pantry. 'They must work with mirrors, or something. Come and see.'

One eye scrunched shut, Flip peered through the glass and saw the back garden. He blinked and saw the front pavement. Another blink and he could watch the television in the sitting room. Speechless, he pulled back and read the careful letters engraved into the brass, 'M. Weston, 1922'.

'I'm afraid the toaster's had it, but everything else works.' Mr Sparrow glanced over his shoulder and found three glum faces. 'Hey! We Sparrows stick together! I'll start baking tomorrow . . . What's this?'

A button. Bim squawked. 'Don't touch it, Dad!'

Mr Sparrow read the label. ' "To cool a cake. Press once for full force, twice for gentle breeze." Interesting . . .'

He pressed the button once and ducked as an iron hand sprang from the wall, a wooden fan in its fist. The fan sliced the air with frightening speed. Gale-whipped, everything not nailed down sailed into the hall. Tea-towels and cornflake packets flew overhead

11

and Bim lunged at the button. Stabbed it. The hand hinged back into the wall.

Silence. A cornflake popped on to the hall carpet.

'Dear me,' Mr Sparrow said. 'Dear, dear me.' Then he laughed. 'We'll have to stop touching the buttons. Flip, remind me not to touch the buttons.'

'Yes, Dad.'

'And tomorrow I start to bake.'

Flip nodded. 'We'll be OK. I'll get a paper round or something.'

His dad stopped laughing. 'Flip, don't be silly. I'd rather you made some friends before you worry about paper rounds. I want you both to be happy here.'

Flip had been a paper boy in London. When his mum and dad had been made redundant, they had had to sell things to pay their bills. He had sold his bicycle to help out. After that, he had managed his round on foot, watching his friends speed past and feeling more and more shy of them. He had not wanted them to see how broke he was.

Bim nipped his arm. 'Come on, let's go outside.'

She was right. Their mum and dad wanted to talk, alone. Flip followed her across the yard to the back garden. A high brick wall surrounded it and Flip pulled a face. 'I don't think I like this. It's like a prison garden.'

'You've never been in a prison garden, Flippy Long Legs.' Bim threw herself on to the grass next to the pond and added another stain to her T-shirt. 'There aren't any fish!'

'We could try to save up for some . . .'

'You could win some,' said a voice.

Flip spun around as a dark face popped over the

12

wall. Blue and silver beads rattled from a fringe of black plaits.

'I wasn't listening.' The girl struggled for a safe grip. 'I mean I was, but I didn't want to. You can win fish on the Prom. I'm Maxie Christian.' Maxie's foot hooked over the bricks and she hauled herself on to the wall.

'Well . . .' Flip started.

'I'm Bim. Come on down and talk.' Bim ran across the lawn. 'Come on, I'll catch you.'

'No, I'm all right. Just stand back.' Maxie swung clear and landed, knees bent, like a paratrooper. She bobbed straight up, giggling. 'When Mr Sparrow said his family were coming, I hoped there'd be someone for me. I mean . . .' Her hand twisted into her plaits. 'I mean, someone my age.'

'I know what you mean.' Bim grinned at her. 'This is my brother, Flip. It's Philip, really, and I'm Beverley, but everyone calls us Flip and Bim.'

'I'm Maxine, but everyone calls me Maxie.'

'I love your hair!' Bim touched one of the silver beads.

'They feel funny if you're running.' Maxie nodded and the blue beads clattered against the silver ones. 'The plaits are "cane rows" and they take ages . . . I don't suppose you'd show me all the magic stuff, would you? I've never dared ask, before.'

Bim and Flip looked at Maxie's shy smile, then at each other. Flip swallowed. 'Magic stuff?' he said.

Maxie's eyes widened. 'Didn't you know? It's a magic shop.'

'I thought it sold plants!'

'Oh, it sells those as well, but mostly it sells magic stuff. You know, cards and crystal balls and things. That's much better than plants.'

13

Five minutes later, Mrs Christian arrived with Maxie's brothers, Devon and Carl, and a massive strawberry flan. Flip looked at the Christians' clothes and embarrassment knotted his middle. Maxie's T-shirt matched her blue beads, her brothers wore expensive trainers and her mother's white dress looked brand new. Flip shuffled his feet and hoped that no one noticed his ankles. He had outgrown his jeans, as usual, and his ankle-bones bulged under the hems like marbles. And Bim was just Bim, from red curls to scraped knees to scuffed sandals, a zoo of different smudges.

Mrs Christian smiled. 'I'm Celestine Christian. Welcome to Weston! I hope you like strawberries?'

'We love strawberries!' Mr Sparrow shook her hand. 'That's a lovely way to say hello! It smells home-made.'

'I never use packet stuff. Do you cook?'

'I did, until the factory closed. Anyway, that was months ago.' He put one arm around Bim's shoulders. 'Since then, I've baked ten million wedding cakes and fried in a burger bar.'

'Dad's the best cook in the world.' Bim ignored her mother's glare. 'Are you coming in to look at the magic stuff?'

'Of course she's coming in,' Mrs Sparrow said. 'We haven't had time to tidy up, so . . . What magic stuff?'

Mrs Christian laughed. 'I wondered if you knew. We'll wait until you've settled in.'

'No, please come in. We'll look around together.'

Maxie's brothers had homework to do and excused themselves. They were in their late teens and made Flip feel about five years old. And their trainers were brilliant. He looked at his ankle-bones and sighed.

Then he walked into the shop, for the first time.

The first thing that hit them was the smell of a thousand kinds of herbs and spices. Mix vanilla ice-cream with Christmas dinner stuffing, peppermint and furniture polish and you might have the smallest hint of that smell. Bunches of herbs swung from the shop ceiling, some grassy-green and as dry as burnt paper, others yellow and suede soft.

No one spoke as their eyes found empty tortoise-shells, snakeskins, bottles of oil, candles and statues and silver moons. Piles of cards tilted over old books. Bags of scented charcoal bulged between carved stones and jewels like tiger-eyes on iron chains. A glass bottle pulsed with silvery beetle-shells. Gulping, Flip nearly dropped a jar of twisted root labelled 'mandrake'. His dad opened a drawer and found a black box. Inside, a crystal ball the size of an egg glistened on blue silk. It cost £15.

'Fifteen pounds for a lump of glass!' Mr Sparrow hunched over it, evilly. 'I look into the crystal ball and see. . .! And see. . .! Gordon Bennett, I can see something!'

'Where?'

They crowded around him, squinting into the glass. The first trace of misty fingers beckoned to them.

'David, put it away!' Mrs Sparrow cringed backwards. 'I thought you said your grandad was a nice old man?'

'He was nice,' Mr Sparrow laughed. 'Just a bit crazy.'

Alone for a moment, Flip opened one of the wall-cupboards for a quick peek and yelped backwards. Idiot! They were pot heads, not real ones. Grinning, embarrassed, he wondered why someone would

15

want a white, pot head with black lines all over it. Lower down the cupboard, rows of square drawers the size of match-boxes waited to be explored. Flip reached forwards and cracked his hand on a sheet of glass. A noise like an angry elephant shook the room and a red flag twanged out of the wall . . . 'Stop thief!' in white letters on red.

'Oh, very funny!' Flip rubbed his bruised finger-nails. 'Ha funny ha!'

Next stop, the cellar. The air tasted of dry soil and potatoes and black water glittered in a deep well. Shelves grew out of the walls like fungus, heavy with things that Flip's dad decided he did not want to see. He led a rapid retreat to the kitchen.

'So, we've got weird things in the shop and weird things in the cellar. That calls for a cup of tea.'

Flip tugged Bim's jeans pocket and crept back into the hall. 'Come on Bim—Maxie—I'd go pop if I had any more tea. Let's try the attic.'

They climbed the narrow stairs to find a locked door without a key.

'Brilliant! I wonder where the key . . .? No, that's stupid.' Flip pulled the Key to the Other out of his pocket. 'If it was the key to the attic, it would say "Key to the Attic".'

Bim shrugged. 'Try it and see.'

Flip tried the key in the lock. 'No good. It won't op—' Pins and needles throbbed through his finger tips. Church bells rang between his ears. The door swung wide. '—pen.'

'You can't have turned it properly.' Bim pushed past him. 'Let's have a look around.'

Speechless, Flip stumbled after her.

The attic stretched over the whole shop and bookcases honeycombed every inch of the walls. Sheet-shrouded chests grew a fur of dust.

Flip gazed out of the window, wondering if he was going crazy. Pins and needles and church bells and not a church in sight! Beyond the roof-tops, the two bays of Weston and St Brigid shone silver, the high cliff pushing between them like a crocodile's head. At the tip of the crocodile's nose, the grey stone of a castle caught glitters of sun. Two witch-hat towers stared over the crinkle-mirror of sea.

'That's Weston Point, with the Castle on top.' Maxie pointed to the cliff. 'Weston's on the left and St Brigid's on the right, with all the boats in the Marina. I'll show you around tomorrow, if you like?'

'That would be brilliant!' Flip said. 'How about after breakfast?'

Maxie grinned. 'As soon as I've washed the dishes.'

Bim kicked the largest chest. 'Come on, Flip, it might be treasure.'

'It might be, but it's locked and there's no key.' Flip sat on the lid and swung his legs. 'So hard luck, Bim-Bong, 'cos we can't get it op—' Pins and needles. Church bells. Flip landed, upside down, on a pile of mouldy paper.

'—pen.' Bim said, sweetly. 'You must have popped the lock when you sat on it. It's empty, anyway.'

Maxie found the Key against the wall. 'That's funny. It looks hundreds of years old. If it's older than the lock, how can it op—?'

The wall between the shop and the hairdressing salon vanished and Maxie sat down, her feet in the Sparrow attic, the rest of her in her brother Devon's bedroom. Her brother lay on his bed, a chemistry

17

book in one hand, a spoonful of raspberry yoghurt in the other. His mouth froze in mid-bite.

'I didn't do anything!' Maxie jumped up, not understanding the church bells or the tingle of energy around the Key. 'Honestly. I didn't do anything.'

Bim put her hands in her jeans pockets. 'You've broken the wall.' She said, 'Hi, Devon.'

Devon muttered, 'Hi.' The spoonful of yoghurt blobbed down his T-shirt.

Maxie sniffed. 'I just wondered how an old key could fit a new lock. We've got to do something before anyone finds out. Flip, shut . . . the door.'

The wall was back, solid and dusty and real.

'Weird.' Flip shook his head. 'Weird.'

Bim took the Key. 'All she did was lean on the wall . . .' Bim leant on the wall. 'And it op—'

The wall vanished.

'—pened.'

Devon threw his tub of yoghurt out of the window. 'What are you doing! What's going on! I'm trying to do my homework and you keep knocking the wall down!'

Bim smiled at him. 'Shut,' she said.

The wall shut and Bim handed the Key back to Flip.

'Maxie. This shop sells real magic, doesn't it?' Flip watched Maxie's face. 'That's why you haven't come in before.'

Maxie nodded, glumly. 'Everyone says so. That's how Mum and Dad managed to buy next door so cheap.'

Flip swung the Key on its rope. He felt strange, not sure whether to be frightened or jumping-up-and-down happy. 'Wow! You know, this thing must

18

be worth a lot of money. Everyone will want to buy it . . . Firemen . . . Policemen . . .'

'Burglars?' Maxie said. 'I bet they'd love it. You'd better think before you tell anyone, Flip. If the Government find out, they might take everything magic because it's too dangerous for ordinary people.'

'That's a good point, Max.' Flip suddenly felt a lot less calm. With the Key in his hand, he could be a burglar himself. The thought made him jump and he jammed the Key back into his pocket. 'You'd better ask Devon not to say anything. We have to think about this.' For the first time, he wondered if the Key might bring more trouble than money.

Bim crossed her heart and hoped to die. Then she grinned. 'Now I know why Great-grandad Sparrow said we'd love it here. Isn't this great?'

Flip winced. 'Yeah, really wonderful.'

It was getting dark and the Christians had to leave. As they said their goodnights, a rocket split the sky and shattered in a waterfall of green stars.

'That's Nicholas Weston, launching rockets from the Castle.' Mrs Christian pointed towards the cliff. 'He's a strange boy. His grandma, Grace Weston, is quite a lady. She does a lot for local charities and she's never too busy to come to my meetings.'

'Weston' had been the name on the spyhole in the kitchen, Flip remembered.

'She scares me to death.' Maxie's beads rattled. 'I always thought she was stranger than Mr Sparrow . . . Oh, I mean the old one, not you, Mr Sparrow.'

Flip's dad smiled. 'That's okay. It's nice to know we aren't the only odd bods in the town.'

Flip wondered if they would have laughed so much if they had known he had the Key to the Other in his jeans pocket. When everyone else was asleep, he crept into the shop and used the Key to open the glass wall in the store cupboard. An hour later, he slid into bed with pyjamas full of twisted paper. Each twist held a palm-full of magic—Fixit Dust, Invisible Dust, Smelly Foot Powder, False Measles, Toad Croak. . . . Under the sheets, a torch between his knees, Flip tried a pinch of Smelly Foot Powder.

'Aaaarghhh! Phhoooo!' Flip sprawled out of bed. 'Crrrrughhh! Asphweeeee!'

Somehow, he fumbled the window open and hung out, tears running down his cheeks. His room stank like the inside of an old clog. By the time that it had cleared, he was a lot less tempted to try the shop's magic.

The Hairy Thing

Seagulls squabbled above the cliffs and the sea breeze ruffled Flip's bedroom curtains. It was Monday, his first full day in Weston St Brigid and a holiday. He lived in a magic shop with brass eyes everywhere and buttons and labels. On the wall, his cuckoo clock popped out a wooden dragon instead of a cuckoo. It was fantastic.

Flip washed his feet three times, stuffed the Key into his trouser pocket and whooshed down the carpet slide into the kitchen.

'Morning, Flippy.' His dad cracked eggs into a frying pan. 'Slept well?'

'Fine.' Flip stood up and stretched. 'Must be the sea air. I kept the window op—' Pins and needles. Church bells. Flip gulped. '—en all night.'

Nothing happened and Flip remembered that he had not touched anything, just held the Key in his hand. He would have to be careful where he said 'open'. When no one was looking, he sprinkled a pinch of Fixit Dust into the toaster. To his delight, it twanged, shrugged battered insides and decided to work again.

The Sparrows had started on their second mugs of tea when the oven door crashed back and a small, brown, hairy body leapt out, shrieked and vanished into the hall. Four mugs sank on to the kitchen table.

Flip swallowed. 'Did anyone see what I just saw?'

'You mean the little hairy thing with no clothes on?' Mr Sparrow tried to control his face. 'I think I did. Can we have a vote on this? All Sparrows who saw a hairy thing jump out of the oven, raise their right hand. Yes, in that case I did see it.' He closed his eyes. 'Gordon Bennett!'

Mrs Sparrow staggered out of her chair. 'Where's it gone? What was it?'

Flip had to swallow, again. 'Maybe it was a dog.'

'Not on two legs.' Bim shook her head. 'It had hands, as well. And it was this big.' She held her arms at full stretch. 'You don't get dogs that big.'

Mrs Sparrow sagged against the table. 'It wasn't really that big, was it?'

'No, it wasn't.' Mr Sparrow crept into the hall. 'I can't see anything. Maybe it's in the cellar.' He eased the door open. Something splashed into the well and he grinned. 'Well, well!'

'Dad, it isn't funny!' But Flip had to grin back. 'Anyway, if it's in the well, it'll drown and that's that.' He flinched, a horrible thought in his head. 'Anyway, it's gone. Come on, Bim, we'd better get a move on. Maxie's showing us the town. I wish we didn't have to go. . . .'

Not with Hairy Things running around the house.

Maxie was waiting for them. 'Hi Bim, Flip. I thought I'd show you where school is, to start with. We could walk back through Weston.'

'Sounds fine to me,' Flip said. 'You lead the way.'

A large patch of sand had formed in front of the shop door. Flip kicked it and the patch swirled angrily, drifted backwards and spun away. Without a breath of breeze to carry it, the sand gathered speed and whizzed in a spiral cloud back towards the beach.

Bim and Maxie skipped down the hill, already friends enough to tease each other. However much Flip needed a job for the holidays, he knew that he needed a friend, as well. It would be terrible to spend the whole summer without a boy of his own age to talk to.

At the bottom of the hill, the main Weston Road curled towards the town centre. Flip's mind spun with thoughts of the Key and the Castle and the Hairy Thing in the oven. Five minutes later, he peered at Weston Amusement Park from the top deck of the Prom bus. His toes curled at the big wheel and the speedway, but they would have to wait until he had a job. Or he could sell the Key . . .

The bus stopped at the school gates and Maxie pointed to the different classrooms. She was thirteen, like Flip, so she might be in his class next term. At eleven, Bim would be with the first years.

Baking in the hot sunshine, Flip followed Maxie along the Prom and tried to find a paper-shop that needed a paper-boy. It was too late, the local kids had snatched all the available jobs. Flip pushed the Key around his pocket and tried to hide his disappointment.

'My dad teaches English at the school. And he takes the SLD kids for special lessons.' Maxie hopped over a fallen windsurf board.

'What's SLD?'

'It's something about learning . . .' Maxie frowned. 'Dad always calls it "SLD". They're kids who need extra lessons to read and write. A special teacher gives them three lessons a week and Dad takes another two. He helps coach the cricket team, as well.'

Maxie looked away but Flip had heard the sadness in her voice. His fingers tightened on the Key. 'Your mum and dad work hard, don't they?' And his fingers tingled. He had not said 'open' and there were no church bells, but his fingers had tingled.

'They sometimes don't have much time for me . . .' Maxie stopped walking and stared at him. 'I wasn't going to say that.'

The Key had made her say it.

'That's all right, Maxie.' Bim twanged Maxie's beads. 'You'll just have to be my bestest ever friend. Flip's too, if you want.'

They sat on the rail above the beach, watching the people play volleyball. Every shop on the Prom sold those big, inflatable boats Flip had always fancied. And candy-floss and ice-cream and rock made into false teeth and bananas.

'I sometimes want to buy it all.' Flip pointed at the happy tourists. 'Isn't it stupid? I mean, they're only little things . . . Ice-cream and rock . . . Or those yellow beach-balls. I don't even need a beach-ball. But I'd like to walk into that shop and say "I want a beach-ball" and walk out with one.'

'You can borrow mine any time, Flip.' Maxie touched the sharp bone of his elbow. 'Mum said your dad's factory shut down. It must have been awful.'

'Mum and Dad both worked there, so they both lost their jobs. Dad sells his cakes and Mum does people's typing, but they don't make much. I think I'll sell the Key.' Flip twisted it between his fingers. 'I'll think about it for a bit, but I think I'll sell it. Come on, we'd better go back.'

Mr Crouch, the ice-cream man, collected money at

24

the entrance to the pier, thin face set in its permanent scowl.

'He's ever so rich,' Maxie said. 'He runs the ice-cream vans and he owns the pier. But he wouldn't reduce the entry price for kids and old people until a few years back. Then he only knocked ten pence off.'

Bim snorted. 'He's an old Lemon-Face.'

'Bim!' Flip frowned at her, then giggled. The old man was a lemon-face.

It was a long walk back to the shop. By the time they reached Caliburn Hill, all Flip wanted was a cold shower. His socks scrunched with sand. He did not notice the black car until it skidded towards the main road. Wheels smoking, it shot between two coaches, into the oncoming traffic. This time, Flip remembered and took its number plate—'SET 9'.

'Ouch! That's crazy!' He stared after the car, wondering. 'He was here yesterday, as well.'

'Are you sure?' Maxie looked surprised. 'You mean he was watching the shop?'

'I think so. I wish I knew why.' Flip glanced up the hill towards the shop. 'Hey! Hey, did you see that!'

'What?'

'I don't know . . . I mean, I don't know what it was. Like a spray of water squirting out of our chimney, only it was dark air, not water.' Flip waved his hands around, helplessly. 'Honestly, Bim. It came out of the chimney.'

'Well, I can't see anything.' Bim shrugged. 'Maybe it was dust. Come on, Maxie. Race you to the shop!'

Flip watched them go, red curls and black plaits very close as the girls giggled together. The black car had spun a second set of skid marks across the road. Flip had a very bad feeling about that car. Its driver was up to something.

Inside the shop, Mrs Sparrow wrapped scented candles in tissue paper and scowled a 'go away!' as Flip peered through the door. Opening the door rang a brass bell and the three customers turned to look at the two red-haired faces staring in at them. Flip managed a watery grin and shut the door again.

'I think we'd better go through the yard.'

Bim scratched the back of her neck thoughtfully. 'Maybe they were in fancy dress?'

Flip thought about the three customers' purple robes and flat hats. 'Maybe they weren't,' he said.

Egg salad for dinner, a Flip favourite. The metal hand fanned on 'gentle breeze', keeping the kitchen cool. By timing his duck, Flip dodged under it and read the inside of the iron elbow. 'Mortimer Weston, 1927.' That name, again.

Even on 'gentle breeze', the hand sometimes forgot and wafted too hard. A slice of tomato blobbed on to Bim's jeans. She peeled it off, blew on it and gulped it down. Flip wolfed a lettuce sandwich and his mother groaned.

'Manners, you two! Flip, don't eat so faaaaaaaaarrrrghh. . .!'

A hairy body rocketed out of the oven, landed on the table and drained the milk jug in one gulp. Its feet sank into the butter and skidded, scattering plates. Hard-boiled eggs bounced on to the floor and Mrs Sparrow's knees vanished under a landslide of lettuce.

'David! It's that Thing again!'

Mr Sparrow leapt for a hairy arm, missed, and thudded on to the table.

The Hairy Thing screeched with laughter and the strawberry flan catapulted into the sink.

'One hundred and eighty!' Flip yelled. 'Bim, head

26

it off . . . It's running for the cellar, again.'

Bim tore the cellar door open, leapt inside, and froze. Flip skidded next to her, and froze. His mum and dad froze behind him.

'Dwarfs,' his dad said. 'We've got dwarfs in the cellar. We've got a Hairy Thing in the oven and dwarfs in the cellar. Let's go back to London.'

Four grey-bearded dwarfs swung picks into the cellar wall. Their loose coats flapped open to show orange, goose-webbed feet.

'I think they're wonderful!' Bim's eyes shone. 'Aren't they wonderful!'

Flip winced. 'Yeah, just brilliant. I'd better make a cup of tea.'

Bim squelched after him over the crushed lettuce and egg. And gulped. 'Flippy!' Her nails dug into his arm.

'Oww! What's that f. . .?'

'Something's coming out of the tap.'

A solid lump of water squeezed out of the tap, not dripping or splashing but expanding like a balloon, growing bigger and bigger and having to bend at the waist because it was taller than the ceiling. It burbled and slurped and grew into a massive . . . wet . . . man.

The water-man slopped on to the floor. Its water body swirled and made mini-rainbows in the light from the window. Water-white eyes peered at Flip, then through their own, transparent head to the door. The water splashed, reared up and squelched out of the keyhole to the yard.

'Flip! There's another one starting!'

'No way! No way . . . Get back in there! Get back. . . Wet. . . thing. . .!'

Flip fought the wet lump, heaving at the new

water-man's big toe until it gurgled back into the tap. He stuffed a kitchen scourer into the hole and tied the dish-cloth around it to keep it there. Bim was already through the door and into the street. Ahead of her, a twenty-foot-tall water-man splurged and dribbled his way on to the pavement.

'What's the mat . . .?' Maxie spluttered under a wave of tap water. 'Urgh . . . Bim . . .!'

'Come on, Maxie! Don't let it get away!'

'What is it?'

Bim grabbed her hand. 'Don't talk, run!'

The girls raced down the road, Flip in pursuit and the water-man pouring ahead of them. As the man ran, water spattered the houses and rained onto the road. His feet skated the pavement incredibly fast.

'I think he's shrinking!' Flip gasped. 'Everything he touches gets wet. . . Hey, look out!'

Two elderly ladies turned, saw the water monster, and squeaked in horror. A wall of water exploded around them. For a moment, a shapeless wave rolled around the corner on to the steep part of the road. It pulled back into arms and legs, tall back and sparkling-crystal head.

'Flip!' Maxie lengthened her stride to keep up with him. 'Flip! What are we going to do . . . if we . . . catch him?'

Flip had no idea. 'Just keep running!'

Bim shrieked 'Flip! Be careful. The road!'

Flip dug his feet into the pavement, forgot about the water and slid feet-first into a waste-bin. The wire mesh skinned his ankle and he yelped. Then he scrambled up, waving his arms at the rush of cars.

Two cars hit the water-man from opposite directions. Water cracked apart, filling the sports-car to

28

the brim, and the cars thudded together to block the road.

'It's heading for the sea! Come on Bim!'

The wave waterfalled onto the beach, then slurped back into a running man. Over the warm sand, just before the white edge of foam, a boy stood alone, gazing out over the water. He balanced on one leg, carefully touching his right elbow to his left knee.

'HEY!! Look out!!' Flip stumbled and lost a shoe. 'Hey! You . . . The boy on one leg!'

The boy's blond head turned and met a crashing fall of water.

All down the hill, people had screamed or goggled or rooted to the ground in terror. The boy on one leg said, 'Oh great!', rolled his eyes and took the water full in the face. A tidal wave crushed him into the beach. Two seconds of raging foam and the water man glugged back into shape, five feet tall and bounding from wave to wave like a gymnast. The boy sat very still, drenched, bruised and up to his waist in the sea-froth.

Flip pushed the ginger fringe out of his eyes. He felt stupid. 'You OK?'

The boy raised one brow. 'Is he with you?' He pointed to the vanishing water-man.

'Well, sort of. Are you sure you're all right?'

'I'm not all right, I'm all wet,' the boy said. 'I haven't seen one of those before.'

'No.' And Flip could think of nothing else to say.

The boy stood up and wrung some of the water from his shirt. A copper bracelet glinted around his left wrist and made a green mark on his skin. As Flip watched, another wave broke around his ankles, brown with sand.

Before Flip could stop himself, he started to giggle.

29

'Sorry . . . I'm sorry . . .' He gurgled and punched himself in the stomach and managed to stop. 'It came out of our tap,' he said.'

The boy nodded. 'I suppose it would.'

The boy had the poshest accent Flip had heard in real life and he looked very, very fit. His body was hard and tanned like a tennis player. Even wet through, his hair shone gold and made his dark eyes seem even darker. Maxie had recognized him. She twisted one hand into her beads and passed Flip his missing shoe. When the boy's purple-black eyes frowned at her, she jumped.

'Do I know you?' he asked. 'Mattie or something?'

Maxie studied her feet. 'It's Maxie. My dad's Mr Christian . . . Your reading teacher.'

A cool breeze touched the boy's clothes and he wrinkled his nose. 'I really am wet. You'd better come to my place while I change. It's not far.' He turned and walked away.

Maxie swallowed. 'To the castle?'

'Well, that's my place, isn't it? You don't have to come.'

'Oh, we'll come.' Flip trotted after him. 'Sure, we'll come. I've always wanted to see a real castle.'

The boy shrugged. 'That's a pity. It isn't real.'

The Castle

Flip waited for an explanation. He was still waiting when they reached the path to Weston Point and the two-towered castle in the trees.

'I'm Flip Sparrow, by the way. That's my sister, Bim.'

The boy glanced at Bim. 'Oh,' he said.

Bim's brows bunched together and she dug Flip in the back. Flip ignored her, his long legs easily matching the blond boy's stride. 'Why isn't the castle real?'

'What?'

'You said the castle wasn't real . . . Didn't you?'

'I might have,' the boy said. 'It's only Victorian. Someone burnt the Old House down so they built the castle. Sparrow . . .' He frowned. 'Are you from the shop?'

'We've only been here a couple of days,' Flip admitted. 'And ever since we moved in, funny things have happened.'

'Well, it's a funny shop.'

The boy's bare feet ate the path. Some of the stony patches must have hurt but he never slowed down or complained.

'You haven't told us your name,' Flip said. 'I suppose your family works for the Westons . . .?'

31

'My family are the Westons. I'm Nicholas Weston.' The boy looked back at him. 'Ask Mattie.'

A blush spread out of Flip's shirt, up his neck and into his ears.

Maxie hung her head. 'Sorry, Flip. I should have told you.'

'You should have! I feel a right wally!' Flip kicked a rock over the cliff edge. 'Is he always this friendly?'

'Until you get to know him. Dad says he's really clever, it's just hard for him to read and write. He's dyslexic, so he doesn't see words like we do. And he sometimes forgets things.'

'Like your name?' Flip asked.

Maxie suddenly smiled. 'That might have been on purpose.'

'You like him!'

Maxie wriggled and chewed her lip.

'You do!' Flip grinned at her. 'Maxie likes Nick!'

'Shut up! He might hear you! Shut up, or I'll tell everyone about that water thing coming out of your house.'

Flip remembered the water-man and his grin faded. 'That was really funny. And we've got dwarfs in the cellar and a Hairy Thing in the oven . . . I wish I hadn't messed around with that magic stuff.'

Bim decided that Nicholas Weston was rude. For one thing, he walked too fast and she had to run to keep up with him. She wanted to talk and he knew it and he ignored her. Her bottom lip stuck out.

'I thought only old people wore copper bracelets.' She waited for him to get mad. 'It looks really stupid on a boy.'

'It would look more stupid if I got lost. It's to tell me which way's left.'

Bim frowned. 'Don't you know? Only babies can't tell right from left.'

Nick stopped walking. 'Only babies stick their lips out. You look like a camel.'

Bim sucked her lip back in. If he had smiled, she would have laughed with him, but he did not smile. 'I'm glad our water-man hit you!' she said.

Nick looked at her, really hard. 'It's a shame it didn't hit you. You need a bath more than I do. Egg salad . . . jam on bread . . . chocolate ice-cream. Your jeans are a walking menu.' His eyes turned Bim's face as red as her hair. 'Anyway, Bong, now we know how we feel. Come and meet Grandma.'

Bong? Bim cringed. 'It's Bim!' she said, but he had already gone.

Through a gap in the bushes and the castle rose above them, all grey stone and black-hatted towers, carved lions holding the gutters and a huge, wooden door.

Out of breath, Flip pointed to the castle walls. 'That looks patched . . . Was it bombed in the war, Nick?'

Nick shook his head. 'Bombs wouldn't hit it. Most of it's spell damage.'

Spell damage? Flip's mouth had fallen open when an old man pushed a wheel barrow on to the lawn. The man scowled at Nick. 'You back, then?'

'No.' Nick walked past him and ignored his angry mutters. 'That's Hopkins. He doesn't like me, much, but he's a good gardener.'

'Nicholas? Is that you?'

'I've brought some people, Grandma,' Nick said.

The beautiful voice belonged to an old lady with a basket of herbs on one arm. She walked with a green wooden cane and she had Nick's purple-black eyes.

'Let's see if I know who you are . . . Maxine, of course.' The old lady smiled at her. 'I hope your parents are well?'

'They're fine, thanks, Mrs Weston.'

'And I'd recognise the Sparrow red hair anywhere.' Mrs Weston nodded to Flip. 'You must be Philip and Beverley.'

White hair swept into a bun at the back of Mrs Weston's head and a copper brooch fastened her blouse. The carved head of her stick shone copper, as well.

Finally, Mrs Weston looked at her grandson. 'You usually take your clothes off to swim, Nicholas.'

'I didn't swim. Their water-thing hit me.'

Her brows rose. '"Water-thing"?'

Nick shrugged. 'Ask them.'

'It came out of the tap!' Bim said. 'It was huge! Like a man, but water.' She sneered at Nick. 'It knocked him over and he got wet.'

'I see.' Mrs Weston's mouth curled. 'A man made out of water?'

'It was this big!' Bim stretched both arms.

'It was this big.' Nick's arms made a man half the size and his voice was pure Bim.

'It sounds like a type of water sprite,' his grandma said.

'Well, whatever it is, it's really weird.' Flip frowned. 'Everything was all right, yesterday, then Wham! We've got a Hairy Thing in the oven, dwarfs in the cellar and water-men coming out of the tap.'

'It is strange . . . Wait!' She looked up, quickly. 'Sorath's coming to see you.'

Flip gasped as powerful wings flapped overhead, folded and dropped from the sky. Curved talons glinted shut on Mrs Weston's shoulder.

34

'This is Sorath.' Mrs Weston spoke quietly, letting the bird get used to the strangers. 'He's a sparrow hawk.'

'He's really neat . . .' Then Flip remembered something. 'Mrs Weston, do you know what this word means? It was on a car's number plates. "Set" . . . That's S—E—T.'

'Set?' She frowned. 'I'm not sure it means anything, Philip.'

'Of course it does,' Nick said. 'He was an Egyptian god. He killed his own brother.'

Mrs Weston lifted her stick to stroke the bird's wing. 'I didn't know you'd learnt Egyptian mythology at school, Nicholas.'

'We haven't,' Nick said.

Dark Weston eyes met dark Weston eyes like velvet meeting velvet. Their eyes had no light in them at all.

'Do you like computers, Flip?' Nick asked. 'I've got one inside.'

Flip gulped. 'You've got your own? Can I see it?'

'If you like. I suppose Bong and Maxie want to see it as well.'

Bim glared at him. 'Bim! It's Bim!'

But Nick had gone. The front door opened and Flip trotted through. Later, he remembered that no one had touched the door and the iron handle had not moved. It had simply opened to let Nick pass.

Inside, the castle echoed with emptiness. The few chairs looked antique and the curtains were transparent with years of washing.

Nick watched Flip's brows rise. 'Most of the furniture's from the old house, so it's ancient.'

'I thought your Old House burned down?' Flip said.

'It did. But everything inside was all right.'

Nick's room was huge but Flip's eyes jumped straight to the computer centre. Different shelves held the disc-drive, the VDU and the dot-matrix printer. The paper-box sat in a wire tray, near the floor.

'It's like a dream!'

Nick towelled his hair, shrugging. 'You must have funny dreams.'

'What's this for?' Bim waved a card with a slit cut out.

Maxie took it away from her. 'You put it over a line of writing. It helps you follow the words.'

A stone with a hole in the middle hung from Nick's bed-post.

'I'd hate it here.' Bim shuddered. 'It's like being at school.'

'If you don't like it, get lost.' Nick sat at the computer terminal. 'No one's making you stay.'

Bim mouthed 'stupid' behind his back, but looked over his shoulder, anyway. 'I wish we'd got one of these. I'd do my sums on it and play Space Chase.'

'Ask for one next Christmas.' Nick pushed two discs into the drives and switched the terminal on. The grey metal beeped and groaned. Then Nick stiffened. 'What's wrong now?'

Maxie bit her lip. 'They cost a lot of money, you know. Not everyone can afford them.'

The green letters danced in everyone's eyes but not in Nick's dark ones. He slowly touch-typed the commands and the screen blacked out. A new file opened and he typed along the top line:

'My name iss Nicholas weston and i m dyslexic sometimes I frget ot think and put my fut in my mouth. Sory, flip and bong.'

'Why were you standing on one leg, on the beach?' Flip asked.

'It's hard for me to tell left from right, so anything like that's really difficult. I practise a lot.'

'What about the rockets?'

'They tell people where we are,' Nick said. 'People come to look around the library or to hide where it's safe. You can see the rockets for miles.'

'Couldn't you just give them your address?'

'That would be boring.' Nick stood up. 'Anyway, I like to go into Great-grandad Mortimer's tower to see his old inventions.'

'Can we see?' Bim asked.

Nick shrugged. 'If you like.'

And Flip stiffened. Mortimer Weston! 'Nick, did he do things for the shop? You know, brass eyes and iron hands and things?'

Nick looked at him so blankly that Flip blushed and spluttered and tried to shrink to a metre tall. When he stopped cringing, Nick had walked away.

Mortimer Weston's invention room crouched under the witch-hat roof of the left tower. The spiral staircase tasted of smoke and bad eggs.

'He set fire to it a lot,' Nick said. 'Come on, it isn't far.'

Trudging after him, already pink and sweating, Bim aimed a fist at his back. And missed. 'Hey! Slow down! You're always rushing around.'

By the time that they staggered out of the stone spiral, they were gasping and dripping. Not Nick. His face glowed with spare energy.

'Guess which way in.'

Flip followed Nick's finger to the two identical doors across the landing. 'All right, I guess the one on the right.'

Nick stepped aside. 'Try it.'

If it had been locked, Flip had already decided to open the door with the Key and watch Nick's reaction. To his surprise, the door opened easily. He looked through and saw Nick on the other side. Nick, Bim and Maxie, looking in at him. Flip backed away and closed the door, twisted around as fast as he could . . . And Nick and Bim and Maxie were still there, behind him.

Flip swallowed. 'It must be the other one . . .'

This time, he grabbed the door's handle and leapt through. And landed on the gravel drive in front of the castle. Frozen, Flip gaped at the lawn and the tree-tops. A hand caught his wrist and pulled him backwards and he was in the tower again.

'Hard luck, Flip. Wrong door.' Nick smiled, pityingly. 'Follow me this time.' He walked towards the wall between the two doors and it opened in front of him.

Maxie grinned. 'Never mind, Flip.'

They walked into a circular room littered with failed experiments. Flip picked his way over coils of hose, tangled cable and balls of waste paper, trying to find empty space to stand in.

Nick pointed to a squashed penny-farthing bicycle with wings and a broken umbrella. 'That's the weather machine. Great-grandad Mortimer was dyslexic, as well. It runs in our family. But he was our only inventor. The weather machine was his favourite.'

Flip blinked at the flattened bicycle. Wings made of crushed tins sagged against the frame. Above them, the battered umbrella dangled ripples of wire to a box taped to the bicycle seat.

'It's full of magnets.' Nick tapped the box. 'And solar power zaps through the wings. Put them together and you control the weather.'

'It looks brilliant.' Flip tried to sound impressed.

'It doesn't work.' Nick sat on the table edge. 'None of Mortimer's ideas worked. They were all for fun.'

Flip's eyes widened. 'Hey, I could try some Fixit Dust on it . . .!'

'No you couldn't! Don't fool around with things like that. Magic isn't a toy. . .' Nick stopped himself.

'What do you know about that?' Flip asked. 'Nick . . .?'

'About what?'

'About magic!' Flip groaned. 'Come on, you know what I mean.'

They might have argued but the colour suddenly leaked out of Nick's face. Flip thought all of that charging up stairs had caught up with him. He left Nick to rest and clambered on to the window-sill overlooking the far side of Weston Point. Beyond the trees, he glimpsed a mass of crossing paths.

'One of those drops right on to St Brigid's Rock.' Nick struggled on to the sill and rested his head on the glass. 'It's a killer.'

Outside the window, a small mirror revolved on an iron chain.

'Nick, what's that for?'

'It bounces . . .' Nick swallowed and decided to keep talking, this time. 'It's an old superstition. It's supposed to reflect spells.'

That was it! Nick had talked about spell damage. He had known about Fixit Dust. His family's last house had burnt flat without losing any furniture and people attacked it with spells. Nicholas Weston knew something about magic and Flip was going to find out how.

'What's in the other tower, Nick?'

'What other tower?'

Flip nearly screamed. 'Nick . . .!'

'Just books.' Nick jumped down from the window. 'It's getting dark. You'd better go now.'

Mrs Weston came into the garden to say goodbye. Sorath had flown to the cliffs and Bim sulked.

'See you tomorrow, Nick?' Flip asked.

Nick shrugged. 'You might. I suppose I could bike to your shop.'

Someone else with a bike. Flip sighed. It might be years before he could save up for one.

Mrs Weston smiled at him. 'You know, Philip, the Sparrows have been in Weston almost as long as we have. Our families have always been friends. Goodbye, for now. I'm sure I'll see you all very soon.'

They walked down the drive, Bim still sulking, Flip thinking.

'I think I like her, now.' Maxie pointed towards the castle. 'And I love that hawk.'

Bim nodded. 'That was the best thing in the place.'

'Just because Nick can do your voice.' Flip remembered the look on her face and grinned. 'Serves you right for being rotten to him.'

'I hate him.' Bim kicked the gravel. 'He's no fun. He's another lemon-face. He's . . .'

'He's very lonely.' Maxie stopped walking. 'And you were rotten to him, Bim. Your water thing could have hurt him and he could have been mad about it. But he wasn't. He was good about it.'

Bim sniffed. 'I don't care. I still hate him.'

* * *

40

Three o'clock in the morning. Waking up suddenly, Flip wondered where he was. He heard a lorry door slam and voices. Too sleepy to get out of bed, he squirmed up the mattress to the brass eye. This time, it gazed into the yard, turning it as bright as day, and showed Flip's mum and dad in their dressing gowns talking to a small Chinese man with a round hat and nails a foot long. Mr Sparrow forced a smile and unrolled a parchment scroll, ticking off the list of new stock for the shop. Silent figures carried bunches of herbs, silk packets and bamboo boxes of magic through the kitchen door. When the lorry finally drove away, Flip saw his dad's mouth move . . . 'Gordon Bennett!'

The Great Typhon Qabahl

Nick cycled to the shop the next morning, pretending to be bored and ignoring Flip's grin. 'I'm riding down to the beach. I suppose you could sit behind me . . .'

'Dangerous.' Devon had been listening from the salon door. 'Flip's legs are too long. How about borrowing my bike, Flip?'

Flip stared at him. 'Are you serious?'

'Sure, why not? I'll go get it.'

'That solves that,' Nick said. 'Now all you have to do is put your shoes on. I'm not going anywhere with your feet sticking out.'

After ten separate washes and a pint of deodorant, Flip's feet still gave the odd whiff of Smelly Foot Powder.

'OK, wait here and I'll find my trainers.' He ran into the shop.

'Where are you going?' Bim had taken a fancy to the dwarfs and was taking them a tray of breakfast. 'Is Maxie here?'

'No, Nick is. We're going to the beach.' Flip realized that he was grinning like an idiot. 'You and Maxie could meet us, later.'

'All right. But if he's rude I'll thump him.' Bim kneed the cellar door open. 'And your feet still smell horrible.'

As Flip sneaked back through the shop, a little girl bought a packet of spiders'-web sticking plasters and seaweed paste that glistened like green treacle. Through the window, Nick and Devon talked bicycles.

'What are you grinning at?' Nick demanded.

'Just glad you've come, I suppose.' Flip swung on to Devon's bike, then groaned as Nick did not bother to wait. 'I knew he'd do that!'

Devon nodded. 'So did I!'

It was great to be on a bike again, and Devon's bike was better than Flip's old one. Weston Bay hung below the roofs of the houses, bright white and dotted with sail-boards.

'Nick, where're we going to leave the bikes?' Flip pumped the pedals until he caught up. 'I don't want someone nicking it.'

'There's a rack outside the swimming pool, if you're worried,' Nick said. 'And if you don't stop grinning, I'm going home.'

With the sun up and the schools on holiday, people had flocked to the baths. Flip padlocked Devon's bike to the rack. Two metres away, a patch of sand bubbled into an eye with sand eye-lids and a sand pupil focusing on the two boys. Then it melted into a footprint that ran along the sea-wall, back to its master to tell him that the boy had come.

A new stall squeezed between the burger stand and the postcard seller. Above the curtains and painted backcloth, gold letters gave the magician's name. The Great Typhon Qabahl.

Flip blinked. '"The Great Typhoon Who?"' He shouldered a path through the crowd, feeling Nick follow. '"The Great . . ."'

'Typhon Qabahl,' Nick said. 'I don't know who he

is but I know his name. I just know things, Flip. Look, there he is.'

Of course, Flip looked. If someone says 'Look!' you look. Flip noticed two things—the stage was ankle-deep in sand and a pair of footprints pressed into it, centre front. As if someone was standing there. Someone invisible.

A sudden fizz of sand and black smoke poured from the footprints, black sparks startling squeals and laughter from the audience. Flip did not laugh. The Great Typhon Whoever ran violent eyes over his audience and his face was as white as cheese. And Flip had seen it before.

The show started with thunder-flashes and clouds of smoke. Magic wand in hand, the man spun between tables piled with props and conjured different coloured fire from a line of empty bottles. Another flash and he opened a box to reveal not a pretty pigeon but a baby crocodile.

'That's a funny wand,' Flip said. 'It's too long.'

And wrong. Dead wrong. One end of the black wood was silver and sharp enough to skin a sausage.

Volunteers trooped on stage and laughed as the magician picked their pockets without them feeling a thing. They squeezed back into the audience and Qabahl pointed to his left wrist. Five volunteers found empty space where their watches should have been. Red-faced, they went back and Qabahl made them ask 'pretty please' for their things.

'He'd keep them, if he could,' Flip said. 'That's not an act.'

'And now, ladies and gentlemen . . .' Qabahl smiled. '. . . boys and girls. From the deserts of Egypt I give you the magic of the sands.'

44

The stick twirled and a heavy, dark mist seeped from the sand. Behind it, Qabahl moved like a killer cat. Black fire gushed from the floor of the stage and in it was the face of a giant crocodile. Another twirl of the stick and the sand rippled, rising in a solid wave that sprouted stubby arms, tooth-filled snout . . . A sand crocodile heaved its body through the mist.

'Nick . . .!' Flip shivered and had to swallow. 'That's amazing! That's the best magic I've ever seen!'

'It's the worst,' Nick said. 'Those aren't tricks, it's real.'

Flip stared at him. 'It can't be!'

'Don't be stupid! You live in the Sparrow shop, you know it's real. And he hates Grandma . . . all of the Westons.' Nick bit his lip, angrily. 'I just know, Flip. Trust me and let's get out of here.'

Nick was trying to worm backwards. And then Flip saw the back of a car parked beside the burger stall and the number-plate 'SET 9'.

'Nick! He's the man from the shop—. From the car, I mean.' Flip's voice drowned in happy laughter. 'Nick!'

Flip pinched Nick's arm to make him turn. As he did, the crowd stopped clapping and a hot voice cut through him.

'A volunteer! Give him a big hand, ladies and gentlemen!'

With a bump of packed bodies, the crowd swept Flip sideways. A space of terrible emptiness surrounded Nick and the Great Typhon Qabahl beckoned him towards the stage. Dark eyes narrowed, Nick gave a quick nod as if he had decided what to do and walked up the steps. Qabahl towered over

45

him like a burnt tree, all black suit and thin, crooked elbows.

'Now, are you going to tell us your name?' Qabahl smiled with his teeth. 'You do have a name, don't you?'

The audience laughed, good-humouredly.

'You know my name,' Nick said. 'But if you want to play games, it's Nicholas Weston.'

The man winked at the crowd. 'There's always one! Come on then, Nicholas . . . Or do your friends call you "Nick"?'

'My friends do.'

The wand slashed the air and black cloths fell from the back of the stage, revealing a board covered with words.

'You can read, can't you, Nicholas?'

Nick stiffened. 'I can read.'

'All right, then, let's all hear you. The magic words are on the board.' Qabahl turned to the audience. 'And no cheating!'

A few people laughed, but most frowned, not catching the joke. Whatever language Qabahl had written on the board, it was not English.

Nick flinched. 'It's too far away. The letters won't keep still.'

'Oh come on, Nicholas! Or can't you read at all?'

'No, I can't.' Trembling, Nick made himself stand tall. 'I can't read that. You know I can't.'

'No?'

The wand stabbed the board and split it and Nick flinched away. He clutched his shoulder and Flip had sniffed the burnt-burger smell too often not to recognize burned flesh.

Qabahl howled with laughter. 'Of course you can't, you little idiot! It's ancient Egyptian. You're so thick

46

you can't even tell the difference between English and Egy—'

'I can't read it but I know what it means!' Nick yelled. 'You're a thief and a liar. And you cheat at magic. Because you steal it!'

Nick spun and kicked the first table flat. A sandy skid and he toppled the second one. Bottles shattered as if the sand was iron and a terrible, sickly smell gushed from the broken glass. The baby crocodile scampered for freedom and the first scream rang out as people staggered backwards. Crushed helpless, Flip saw Nick leap off the stage and run.

'Nick!' No use, too much noise. 'Nick, wait . . .!'

But Nick had gone, sprinting with the speed of total fear or hatred or both. Within seconds, Flip had lost him.

More than empty bottles had smashed when Nick kicked the tables. Before the crowd's horrified eyes, the stage itself began to crack. Sand rained through the breaking boards and the curtains shivered into shreds of velvet. At this point, most people simply ran for cover. Curiosity held Flip back. As he watched, everything crumbled, changed colour, lost its shape. From the baby crocodile to the golden paint giving Qabahl's name, everything crumbled into sand.

Forty minutes later, Flip found Nick on the sandy-grass slope above the library. Nick's back was to him but Flip would never miss that dark blond hair. When the sun caught it, it shone gold.

Out of breath and shaking, Flip could hardly speak. The memory of the look on Nick's face had made him run too fast and he had never run in pure panic before. Running scared hurt. 'You OK, Nick?'

'I suppose so.' Nick rubbed the front of his shirt

47

with a wet paper handkerchief and the paper turned red. A burnt circle of cotton surrounded the stab-wound and Flip caught another whiff of scorched skin.

What now? Flip wanted to ask a million questions but he was frightened of the answers. Struggling to slow his breathing, he recognized one of the volunteers from Qabahl's magic act, moaning to his wife.

'. . . I definitely had it when I came off stage. I tell you, Liz, that man's a con artist. I'll bet you anything he's nicked all our watches . . .'

Nick nodded. 'I told you Qabahl's a thief. He'll steal anything. Magic, watches. Anything.'

Counting to ten did not help so Flip counted to a hundred. 'Can I ask you something? I wondered why you . . . I wondered. . . Look, why do you keep doing that?'

'Doing what?' Nick finally looked at him.

'When people talk to you, you look all over the place. What do you think's going to happen? The library won't walk off, will it?' He twisted the Key in his pocket and felt the thrill of power. 'It's like talking to a tennis match.'

'I'm making sure nothing's changed,' Nick said.

'Changed?'

'I have to know where things are.' Nick flinched. 'I don't know why I'm telling you this.'

Flip gripped the Key until it burned. 'Well, tell me, anyway.'

'All right.' Nick took a deep breath. 'I once got lost shopping because they moved the shelves. I knew the door was near the coffee. When they moved the coffee, I got lost.' His fingers dug into the grass. 'Sounds stupid, doesn't it?'

'I don't know.'

48

'I didn't tell Grandma, so why am I telling you?'

'I don't know.'

Nick glared at him. 'Don't know much, do you?' His black eyes stabbed into Flip's brown ones. He stiffened. 'You've got the Key!'

Flip gulped. 'Key. . .?' He gulped again. 'What Key?'

For three long minutes, Nick watched him squirm. Then he shrugged. 'Please yourself.'

'Change the subject,' Flip thought. 'Nick, why do you live with your grandma? Your parents aren't dead or anything?'

'They might as well be.' Nick rolled on to his stomach and rested his chin on his hands. 'They make animal films so they go away a lot. They thought I was stupid because I couldn't learn the alphabet or tell the time or remember where I'd put anything. I was always losing things.'

A police car whizzed past, heading for the fallen magician's stand and the crowd of angry people who had lost their watches.

'My dad had fallen out with Grandma, so I'd never met her. Then a film job came up and my school wouldn't have me back.' Nick closed his eyes. 'My dad didn't know what to do. He wrote to Grandma and she brought me here. She told me I wasn't stupid. When I knew there were lots of people like me, nothing seemed as bad. My parents were glad to get rid of me, anyway.'

'That can't be true!' Flip did not like the cool way that Nick was telling him all of this. 'Nick, it can't be.'

'Why not? I was terrible to them.' Nick opened his eyes and peered into Flip's face. 'You're all right, you're ordinary. Everyone thinks they'd like to be different but it stinks. And it's not just reading and writing. I can tell you how many leaves are on that tree. I know things like that. Lots of things.' He tilted his head towards the library wall. 'My parents send their postcards straight to Grandma. They don't even know I can read.'

Dozy with the heat, a sparrow landed on the library roof and scratched itself. The sounds of cars and seagulls drifted over the parched grass.

'I like your grandma a lot.' Flip let the sun warm his neck. 'And Sorath.'

'You're changing the subject again.' Nick sat up and scrunched the paper-handkerchief into a tight ball. 'Anyway, I don't care if I never see them. I'd rather be on my own.'

Flip sat up as well. 'I'll go if you don't want me here.'

'If you want to go, go.'

Flip choked. 'I didn't say I wanted to go! I said. . . You know what I said! Do you want me to go or what?'

'It's a free country.' Nick shrugged. 'Please yourself.'

A mighty howl and Flip bowled Nick down the slope. Tanned legs spun out of control, blond head bounced on the grass. When Nick landed at the bottom, Flip sat on him.

'You drive me bats!' Words failed him and he bounced on Nick's middle. 'Your eyes aren't real! Why don't your eyes reflect the sun?'

'Don't they?'

'You know they don't!'

'Do I?'

Before Flip could thump him, Nick bunched on to one side. His hard elbow rammed Flip's ribs. He

50

squirmed again, tensed and kicked. Flip met the hard ground in a crushed lump of legs, hooting for breath with bees humming in his ears.

'Are you two fighting?' Bim watched them, hands on hips.

'No, we're playing chess.' Nick batted clouds of sandy grass from his back. 'Flip, make sure you knock all the sand off. It can't get into your place on its own but you could carry it in on your shoes.'

'OK. Wow, my head's spinning!' Flip touched his head to make sure it was still there. 'Hi, Max. Hi, Bim.'

Nick glanced up. 'Hi, Maxie. Hi, Bong.'

Bim's brows met. 'It's Bim! Flip, we've been watching the Punch and Judy. You should have seen the crocodile. . .!'

'It was this big!' Nick imitated her voice and her wide-armed exaggeration perfectly. He watched her stalk off, then turned to Flip. 'I think we've seen enough crocodiles. Do you really want to fight?'

'Do you?'

'No. I'd beat you and you'd be mad all day.' Nick started up the slope. 'I ought to go back.'

Falling had squashed the paper twists of magic into a painful clump in Flip's pocket. When he stood up, one fell on to the grass.

'What's that?' Nick stopped, frowning down at him.

'I can't remember. Hey, let's try it out!'

'Let's not! I mean it, Flip!' Nick backed away. 'Look, you don't know what you're doing. . .' Too late, Nick dodged sideways. Green powder covered his right foot.

'I wonder what it is?' Flip watched Nick's foot. 'Nothing's happening.'

51

'It's just as well . . .' Two steps forwards and Nick rooted to the spot. His right foot croaked. 'Oh no . . .!'

'Now I remember . . . It was Toad Croak.' Flip started to giggle.

'You twit!' Nick stamped away. Step, croak. Step, croak. 'Oh, just great! Really great!'

Helpless with laughter, Flip sagged on to the grass.

'I'll get you for this,' Nick said.

'I'm sorry, Nick . . .' Flip swallowed a giggle and snorted. 'But it sounds like a toad in your shoe!'

This was fun magic. It was just a laugh but it brought the memory of Typhon Qabahl and that was not fun magic. Flip stopped laughing. 'It was really weird, you knowing that writing was Egyptian when you couldn't even read it. . .'

'Who are you calling weird?' Pure black, furious, Nick's eyes burned at Flip's startled face.

Flip's mouth fell open. 'Nick . . . I never said that.'

'That's what you meant, though.' And Nick put his head down and sprinted, past Bim and Maxie and away.

Flip heard the angry strides and even angrier toad croaks and did not want to giggle any more. He came to a decision. Nicholas Weston was going to be his friend, whether Nick wanted to be or not. Groaning, Flip ran after him, his poor feet burning on the hard pavement. He arrived at the bicycle racks as Nick stuffed the chain-lock into the saddle-bag.

'You stopped sulking now?' Flip said.

'Get lost.'

Flip stretched against the swimming-pool wall. 'I don't get lost. Not like some people.'

Nick ignored him, jerked the bicycle out of the rack

and stopped. Stiff as wood, he stared at the handle-bars.

'Nick? What's wrong?' Flip pushed away from the wall and hurried forwards. 'What's wrong?'

'Where's the bell gone?'

'It's right in front of you.'

Nick shook his head. 'No. It can't be there because that isn't the bell side. The bell side's this side.' He touched the copper bracelet on his left wrist. 'That's the side I have to ride on.'

'You mean the left?' Flip tried to understand. 'The bell's to tell you which is the left side, like your bracelet?'

'Which side should it be on? I didn't take this off.' Nick's fingers twisted the bracelet around his wrist. 'I know I didn't.'

'Listen, Nick, you drive on the left side of the road and that's the side your bracelet's on.' Flip said. 'The bell's been moved, that's all. I'll put it back for you.'

As soon as Flip had changed the bell back to the left handle-bar, Nick swung into the saddle. Flip watched him disappear along the Prom and fought a sudden shudder. Bells did not get up and walk along bicycle handle-bars. Someone had moved Nick's bell.

The girls waved from the bus-stop and Flip cycled over to them. Bim scraped candy-floss from her sleeve and pretended not to be interested. More honest, Maxie grabbed Flip's arm. He was going to have bruises all over, tomorrow.

'Nick's bell . . .' he said. 'Someone moved it.'

Maxie blinked. 'What? What bell?'

Flip tried to slow himself down. 'Someone moved his bicycle bell. That's how Nick knows which side of the road to ride on.'

'Maybe someone did it for a joke.' Maxie pulled a face. 'You know what people are like.'

'Why pick on Nick's bike? And it isn't funny enough to be a joke.' His skin crept as he imagined Nick pedalling on to the wrong side of the road. Nick could have been killed.

A deep breath and Flip told Bim and Maxie everything that had happened, about the magician being the man who had been watching the shop and about the real magic and everything turning to sand.

'It's funny,' Flip said. 'A week ago, I would've thought that Typhoon man was a fake. Now I don't know what's real and what isn't. I'll walk back with you and push the bike. We'd better stick together.'

Bim frowned. 'He really scared you, didn't he? That Typhoon man?'

'He's bad,' Flip said. 'And he's after something in the shop.'

The Burglar Button

As Flip and Bim arrived home, two customers left the shop clutching a forest of dried grass and something in a wooden box that stank of bananas. Another dark jet of air sliced out of the chimney.

'Bim!' Flip yelled. 'Look! One of those things!'

And the air clung around the house, heavy as grey steam. The brick walls seemed to breathe the darkness out of their own mortar.

'Oh Flippy!' Bim sighed. 'You'll be seeing ghosts next.'

'That isn't funny!' Flip said. 'Can't you see the dark cloud? The whole place is dark. Oh, forget it! Let's go in. But shake your shoes out first. And not a word about Typhoon Whatsit.'

'You mean because of the sand magic?' She shrugged and dragged her own shoes off. 'OK, I suppose we ought to be careful. You know, if Typhoon's been watching the shop, maybe he knows about the Key.'

Flip did not want to think about that. 'Let's go and see Mumbo.'

Their mum had had a good day and she looked happier than Flip had seen her in months. He sat on the counter and Bim ate an apple while their mum described some of the day's customers. Bim was giggling when Flip noticed a moving pattern of light. Scattered like sequins, the pattern had to be a reflection, but nothing in the shop moved to reflect it. It slid up the wall, over the ceiling, behind the counter and split into three circles of light, shining in each Sparrow face. As it touched Bim's apple, the skin darkened, green and red going brown, ripping away. A gush of black pulp drooled over Bim's fingers on to the floor.

'Ughhh! Flip!' She dropped the apple, cringing. 'It's gone rotten. . .'

The brass doorbell tingled and a plump, pleasant-faced man walked inside. Liquid as water, the sparkles of light poured into his left hand. Amazing cold filled the room. Cold and a sudden, wooden silence, as if the traffic outside the shop-windows had faded to another world. Teeth rattling, Flip knew that he looked at his second magician of the day. And this one frightened him more than Qabahl.

From the shiny toes of his leather shoes to the expensive shoulders of his suit, the man was as neat as a new-made bed. When he smiled, his round mouth made Flip think of fish. Or of sharks, because the panic rose in Flip's stomach in waves. He wanted to run.

'Good afternoon. My name's Solomon Cain. And I believe you're Mrs Sparrow?'

Mrs Sparrow nodded. 'That's right. Can I help you?'

'Oh, I hope so.' Cain's smile chilled the room. 'Mr Sparrow's not about?'

'He's selling his cakes. He bakes them . . . And sells them.' Mrs Sparrow licked numb, cold lips, trying to make them move. 'I'm sorry but it's gone really cold in here. . .' And then she knew. Her mouth snapped shut.

'Has it?' Cain laughed at her pale face. 'Well, let's not play games, then. I think you've got something I want. A Key. . .'

Bim squeaked and Flip trod on her foot. To keep his eyes away from Cain's fishy ones, he stared at the man's plump hands and the thick, gold ring circling the left index finger. Frosty light swam around it, a swarm of microscopic fragments like broken ice in a whirlpool.

Mrs Sparrow looked surprised. A key seemed a fairly harmless thing to ask for. 'I can't remember seeing any keys lying around. What sort of key are you looking for? I mean, what does it open?'

Cain shook his head. 'I don't think you'd like to know.'

The Key hummed between Flip's fingers and suddenly he just had to use it. He wanted to wipe that smug smile off Cain's face.

'Well, I do. Why do you want some old key?'

Its false smile shattered, Cain's face turned as hard as a bullet, shark-mouth rippling in and out of escaping words. 'Because . . .' He grated his teeth, hissing. 'Because . . . It opens doors . . .' His teeth bared and snapped shut.

'Do you know someone called Typhoon? He's a magician.' Flip watched Cain's eyes. 'He likes playing with sand.'

This time, the man did not hesitate. 'He's already here, then? I suppose that makes it more interesting. We can't both get what we want. And what both of us don't want is to have those interfering do-gooders flocking in to pick our bones. . .' He stopped and

57

carefully wiped his mouth with a handkerchief. When he looked back at Flip, it was with the fishy smile. 'But I'm here first, or you wouldn't have the Key in your pocket, would you? Let's start with some money. How much would it take?'

Cain eased a leather roll from inside his jacket. For a moment, Flip thought it was a cigar. It was only cigar-size, held together by a silver ring. In total silence, Cain peeled fiver after fiver from the empty-looking roll. Impossible. The pile on the counter was centimetres high and there was no way so much paper could have fitted inside. But fiver after fiver settled on the counter. The Sparrows watched, fascinated.

Without a sound from its brass bell, without moving its handle, the door opened and Nick's grandmother walked into the magic silence and cold of the shop. Flip was so surprised to see her that he forgot his manners and just stared. Bim opened her mouth to speak but never got the chance. Solomon Cain jerked backwards as if a full-grown dragon had crawled out of the floor-boards.

Mrs Weston did not shout but her voice filled every corner of the shop. 'What are you doing here? You know the contents of this shop aren't for you, at any price.'

Flip's mother frowned at the pile of five-pound notes, then at Mrs Weston. 'I knew it,' she said.

'I think you'd better pick your money up and go, Solomon Cain.' Mrs Weston's fingers moved on the top of her stick. Slowly, the light changed, warming, turning back to sunlight. The cold had gone and she smiled. 'Unless you want me to lose my temper?'

Cain's dead-fish eyes glittered. 'You won't always be here, Grace Weston.' He strode out of the door and slammed it behind him. Before the brass bell stopped ringing, the pile of five-pound notes vanished and Bim's apple sat on the floor, fresh green and gold.

'Was any of it real?' Mrs Sparrow shook her head. 'This place is starting to get to me.'

'It's a shame you had to be frightened like that,' Mrs Weston said. 'But it's the quickest way to learn to be careful. The shop is protected from magic but the more powerful magicians can walk in, if they're their real selves. Old Mr Sparrow knew how to manage them.'

The three Sparrows had huddled together for warmth when Cain turned their world cold. Now, they exchanged miserable gulps.

'Oh dear,' Mrs Weston sighed. 'I'm sorry if I'm spoiling your day. The shop will help you but people like Cain will try to creep in behind your backs. You should never leave the house empty.'

Bim and Flip exchanged glances. Bim mouthed 'Typhoon' and Flip nodded. If Typhoon Whatsit had been watching the house, he was probably going to try to get in as well.

'But that isn't why I came.' Mrs Weston gave Mrs Sparrow her most charming smile. 'I'd like you to do me a very great favour.'

'A favour?' Mrs Sparrow looked confused. 'Well, I'm sure . . . If it's possible, certainly.'

Mrs Weston raised one hand. 'Before you agree, please let me explain. I'd like my grandson to stay here for a few days.'

'Hey!' Flip's eyes lit up. 'That would be great! Please, Mumbo!'

Bim stuck her tongue out at him.

After listening to Flip and Bim argue about Nicholas Weston, Mrs Sparrow knew a lot about him. Her face fell. 'Oh. I'm not sure. We aren't very tidy yet. We've been so busy getting used to the shop.'

'I do understand, Mrs Sparrow.' Mrs Weston smiled and it was such a sad smile that Mrs Sparrow blushed. 'Nicholas hasn't slept away from the Castle since he came to me. He'd feel awkward for a while, but it would be good for him. He wears himself out.'

Flip squeezed his mother's arm. 'Please, Mumbo. I'd look after him. Please. I don't know anyone else, apart from Max. . . Please.'

His mum could never say no to a good 'Please'. She sighed and patted his head. 'All right. Yes, of course, we'd love to have him. He can have the spare bedroom.'

The hall door crashed open and the Hairy Thing skidded on to the counter. It giggled and grabbed a jar of ginseng, ready to throw it on to the floor. And saw Mrs Weston. Her hand clenched around the head of her stick and the Thing squealed and vanished. Flip threw himself forwards and just caught the jar.

'Oh no! Oh no, that horrible Thing! I'm so sorry. It keeps appearing and disappearing. It's driving us crazy.' Mrs Sparrow heard herself babbling and groaned. 'I am sorry, Mrs Weston. . . .'

But Mrs Weston took no notice of her embarrassment, as if she had not even noticed the brown, hairy body on the counter. 'I've got to go but, before I do, I thought you might like to keep this. It is a Sparrow's turn.' She slid a book from under her free arm. In all the excitement, no one had noticed it. Now Flip saw that it was very old, leather with iron hinges. Mrs Weston eased it into his hand. 'Ask Nicholas to write in it, for you. You'll understand when you read it.'

Then she turned away. 'Thank you for agreeing to take Nicholas. Goodbye Philip, Beverley.'

They both muttered their goodbyes and Bim ran to open the door for her. When the door closed, they exchanged shrugs.

'Maybe she didn't see it?' Flip's mum shuddered. 'Horrible Thing! And what's in the book? Is it locked, Flip?'

Flip nodded. 'It is, but that doesn't matter. I'll open it,' he winked at Bim, '. . . somehow.'

Bim frowned. 'Well, I've had enough for one day. I'm going upstairs.'

Flip followed her, waiting for the storm. As soon as they were out of earshot, Bim glared at him. 'Old Wood Face here! Great!'

'Come on, Bim . . .'

'You come on! I don't like him.' She dug her toes into the hall carpet. 'And he doesn't like me.'

'But I do like him,' Flip sighed. 'I know you don't get on, but you've got Max. I tell you what. You can have the Key tomorrow. And try asking someone a question while you're holding it.'

'What for?'

Flip grinned. 'You'll see. Let's open the book.'

Still grumbling, Bim followed him into his room and flopped on to his bed while he used the Key. The iron lock clicked and Flip lifted the heavy cover. Thick, creamy pages, yellowed at the edges, fanned under his fingers. Eyes half shut with the effort, Flip scanned the curled letters on the title page.

'Listen . . . "Booke of Frendshipe. Tayles of Corage and Valor." It must be really old, all the spellings are funny.' Flip turned back to the first, blank pages.

Bim crawled next to him. 'Hey, it's all hand-written. By different people.'

The first entry had faded to brown.

'I gyve this boke to my goode frende Thomas Sparrowe to holde for his lyfe.

William Westone (Aged 12)

Year of Owr Lorde 1542.'

Entry after entry passed down the years between Weston and Sparrow until the last, written in blue ink with blots and smudges.

'Your turn to hold on to the book. To Mortimer Weston from his friend, Freddy Sparrow (Age 11). 6 June 1910.'

That was Great-grandad Sparrow. And Mortimer Weston had made the brass eyes in the shop door and the iron hand that blew tomatoes on to Bim's jeans, in the kitchen.

'Let me see, Flip. Open the book.' Bim reached over him and leafed through the pages. 'Some of this isn't bad.'

The book was filled with stories about brave children. Every ten pages, a beautiful drawing showed snarling dragons, witches with warts on their nose, shipwrecks and magic. Always, a boy or girl proved their courage by helping a friend in danger.

'And now we've got it.' Bim scratched her nose and watched her brother's frown. 'It's a shame Old Wood Face has to write in it. I bet he spells his name wrong.'

'Bim!' Flip groaned. 'Oh, come on. Let's go and help Mumbo with the tea.'

The day seemed to be over. Mr Sparrow drove the van back into the yard, happy to have sold a few cakes and to have met people who might buy some more. The family sat around the kitchen table for a late tea.

'Does that button always glow like that?' Bim

pointed her sandwich at the button marked 'For Burglars'. It glowed dark red.

'No . . .' Mr Sparrow stood up. 'Everyone quiet for a minute.'

Somewhere upstairs, a pair of feet crept over the old carpets. And Flip looked down and saw his dad's shoes. Sand! He had brought sand into the house!

Bim jumped up. 'Dad! Dad, it's burglars. . . Dad, do something!'

'All right,' Mr Sparrow smiled. 'I shall press the button.'

Flip counted. One. Nothing. Two. Still nothing. Thr. . . .

The house rocked under a massive crashing of doors. Something upstairs howled with rage.

'It sounds like a wild animal!' Mrs Sparrow grabbed the breadknife, looked at it, and threw it back on the table. 'David, what is it?'

The animal snarl, again, but Flip had guessed who it was as soon as he had seen the sand on his dad's shoes. His stomach curled. 'It's Typhoon!'

Flip skidded into the hall as the house exploded. Typhon Qabahl ran along the landing, arms clutched over his face to protect it from the flying shoes and deodorant sprays. Bulging pockets showed that he had been busy stealing anything he took a fancy to. As he ran, Sparrow belongings leaked from his pockets—cufflinks, an old brooch like a rose, an empty purse. The house fought back. Qabahl howled as a tube of toothpaste bounced off the back of his neck. He reached the top of the stairs as Flip reached the bottom.

'We've called the police!' Flip heard himself yell. 'Don't you come down here! Don't you dare!'

The rain of objects quickened, jars of handcream

and tins of shoe-polish skimming out of the bed-rooms to pelt Qabahl's head and hunched shoulders. Suddenly, the man did not care.

'The police?' Qabahl threw his head back and crowed with laughter. 'What could they do to me?'

He had a point. Police did not chase magicians. Chewing his lip, Flip tried to think. One of his mother's clogs whacked Qabahl on the chin and the man did not even blink. Then Flip heard something. A wooden clatter and flap of wings and the dragon from Flip's clock flew on to the landing. It swooped, jaws open on a stream of pink flame, and set Qab-ahl's jacket on fire.

Energy cracked down the stairs, driving Flip into his dad's stomach. Above them, Typhon Qabahl quivered, curled in on himself, put his hands on the floor. And shimmered out of shape. Hands clenched into scaley feet. Face stretched into a long snout, stuffed full of teeth. Dark flame lapped over the landing carpet as Qabahl changed into a giant, black crocodile. His heavy tail swung into the wall and shredded the paper to ribbons.

'Gordon Bennett! Gordon Bennett!' Mr Sparrow spluttered, hypnotized. 'It's a croc! A naffing-great croc!'

The red eyes sparked, hot as cigarette-ends, and found the flapping dragon. Flip screamed as the crocodile reared up and snapped the brave dragon into splinters. A terrible, burnt-meat stink drove Flip backwards. Before he could turn to run, deadly heat blossomed at the top of the landing, blackened the wall-paper, curled the potted-plants like black springs. A black ripple of fire poured down the stairs and Flip threw himself on top of his dad, flattening them both to the hall carpet. The hair on the back of Flip's neck singed to powder.

'Tell that to the police!' Qabahl snarled. His clawed feet thundered forwards. A final blast of heat and Qabahl leapt, howling, through the window.

Flip struggled towards the kitchen door.

'No!' His dad rugby-tackled him, dragging him down. 'Wait, Flippy. Don't go after him . . . Gordon Bennett, look at this carpet! The whole thing's scorched. . . We're both scorched!' He rubbed Flip's eyebrows and burnt-hair dust trickled down. 'Listen, Flip, he's either hurt or he's not. Either way, you can wait a minute. And who is he?'

Flip shivered. 'The Great Typhoon Something . . . Typhon Qabahl, with a "Q". He's a magician.'

His dad managed a weak grin. 'No! I thought he was a plumber!'

'We'd better see if he's gone.'

His dad followed him outside. Moonlight sparkled on the shattered glass. Deep-burnt into the turf, crocodile footprints showed where Qabahl had lumbered away, vicious sweeps of grass torn from its roots by his powerful tail. He had smashed through the window on to the verandah roof and vanished into the night.

Nick and the Brownie

Flip was supposed to meet Nick at the pier on Thursday morning. Bim and Maxie went with him and they found Nick waiting, rucksack between his feet on the sea wall.

'Hey, Nick,' Flip said. 'You'll never guess what . . .'

'Our magician tried to burgle you.'

Cheated, Flip spluttered. 'How? Who told you? How do you know?'

Nick sighed. 'Come on, Flip. He wants the Key. Of course he'd try to burgle you. I bet Bong took sand into the house in her sandals.'

'No, it was our dad. . .' Flip bit his lip. That was the second time Nick had mentioned the Key.

'You still pretending you don't know what I'm talking about?' Nick said.

'I suppose it's a bit late for that,' Flip admitted. 'But . . .'

'But you don't trust me.' Nick stood up. 'All right, then, but I'll tell you one thing. You'd better stop messing with the shop magic. It took me an hour to wash that Toad Croak off. Are we bussing or walking?'

'I fancy walking. There's supposed to be a big

yacht in the marina.' Flip stood up and stretched. 'How about it Bim . . .? Nick . . .?'

Bim nodded. 'I love boats.'

Nick shrugged. 'I don't mind.'

The weather men had promised a scorcher. Flip unfastened his shirt and rolled his sleeves up. Nick strode next to him in silence.

'You OK, Nick?'

'I suppose so.'

Flip grinned. 'Is that a "yes" or a "no"?'

'I suppose it's a yes.' Half of Nick's mouth smiled. 'Sorry.'

'What for?'

'For sulking because you haven't told me about the Key. I keep forgetting you aren't used to things yet. And I don't blame you, after Qabahl's show. Then he moved my bike bell . . . He wants me dead, Flip.' Nick twisted away and Flip knew he was embarrassed. 'I was scared stiff.'

'Me too. The thing is, Nick, if I tell you everything, you should tell me everything.' Flip nudged him with a bony elbow. 'Shouldn't you?'

'Maybe.' Nick swivelled and knocked Flip backwards into a hedge. 'I'll race you to the Marina. I want to see that big yacht.'

'Hey!' Flip struggled out of the hedge. 'Cheat! Wait . . .!'

Flip's legs were very long but Nick's legs were very fit. They arrived in St Brigid neck and neck and Flip thought Nick was happy to be with him, in the sun.

The Marina bulged with boats. Fishing boats rocked next to sleek motor launches, rowing boats bobbed past sailing dinghies. In the deep water at the harbour mouth, a massive, white and blue yacht swayed at anchor. Water shimmered around its smooth paintwork. Flip stiffened. Unless he was going bats, the water shimmered more around this boat than the others, as if the shimmers were keeping guard.

'Now that's what I call a boat!' Flip said. 'Look at it! It looks brand new!'

'It's new paint, that's all. You can tell it's older by the rigging.'

'Well, whatever. It's a nice boat.' The air had a fishy, oily tang that Flip could have drunk. 'It's the greatest thing I've ever seen. Funny name, though. I wouldn't call a boat that, would you?'

He waited for an answer. When none came, he frowned and turned. Nick's dark eyes pinned him.

'Flip, I can't read it.'

'I forgot.' Flip blushed. 'Sorry. Can't you see it, at all?'

'Of course I can see it.' Nick squinted across the water. 'I can see the letters but they won't keep still.'

'It's called *The Force of Destiny*,' Flip said. 'And what sort of a creep would call a boat that?'

His eyes moved over the white paintwork to the plump man sunbathing on a padded lounger. One of the shimmers of light rippled up the concrete quay. It touched Nick's shadow and leapt back, flying over the water and back into the golden finger-ring. As Bim and Maxie arrived, the plump man stiffened. Fish-lips narrowed in a grimace, then slipped into their usual, fake-pleasant smile. The man stood and gave a mocking wave.

Nick frowned. 'Who's that?'

'He's called Solomon Cain,' Flip said. 'He came into the shop and your grandma told him to get lost.'

'I'm not surprised.' Nick turned away. 'I don't like him.'

'Neither do I. And he knows Typhoon Whatsit. I don't think they like each other, either.'

Bim sniffed. 'Who would like them? They're both drongoes.'

Five minutes later, a good ten metres away from the water, Nick let the others walk ahead. When he turned, the scattering of reflected light stopped and waited. Nick closed his eyes and whispered three words.

'Oh rats, the sun's gone in!' Bim glared at the sudden clouds. 'Just when my arms were tanning, as well.'

The scatter of light had gone and Nick walked past her, haversack swinging. 'Don't worry, Bong. It'll wear off in a few minutes.'

'What'll wear off?' Bim stared after him. 'How can clouds wear off?'

Nick shrugged. 'Wait and see.'

By the time they reached the shop, the sun burned the pavements like a microwave. Flip pointed at the shop roof. 'Nick, just wait a minute. I keep seeing dark air spitting up and Bim won't believe me. Just wait . . . There! Did you see it?'

A plume of dark air curled from the chimney, split into three and flew over Weston like a trio of rockets.

'Of course I saw it.' Nick's eyes narrowed. 'What have you been doing in there?'

'Nothing!' Flip flinched. 'Well . . . Well, I didn't ask for a black cloud around the roof.'

'I knew it!' Nick shook his head, hopelessly. 'I knew you'd been playing around!'

'I wish I knew what those black spurts were,' Flip said. 'That was the worst one yet.'

Nick had started to follow Bim into the yard when

69

he gasped and twisted so fast that his rucksack nearly broke Flip's chin.

'Don't move! Look!'

Sand on the pavement. Deep sand. It opened into an eye, widened, knew that it had been seen and snapped shut. The sand shrunk into a footprint and Nick leapt on top of it with both heels, scrubbed and scrubbed until the grains wafted apart. Exhausted, he knelt and drew a sign in the sand, a circle with a star in it and a flying bird in the star.

'Now it can't go back to Qabahl and tell him I'm here.' Nick looked up at the three frightened faces. 'Sorry if I made you jump.'

Bim hunched her shoulders. 'We're getting used to it.'

A swift goodbye to Maxie and Flip led Nick into the kitchen. Mr Sparrow stood at the table, wrist-deep in icing sugar.

'You must be Nick.' Mr Sparrow gave him a sticky hand to shake. 'Welcome to the shop that Sparrow built. Flip's talked about you a lot.'

'I bet.'

Mrs Sparrow smiled. 'I hope you won't mind the mess, Nicholas.'

Nick started to say something but they never found out what. A wild shriek and the Hairy Thing shot out of the oven, bounced on to the table and gobbled the marzipan from the top of the cake. Its nails ripped the yellow paste to shreds and stuffed it into its greedy mouth.

Nick sighed. 'A brownie as well as a water sprite. Typical.'

'My icing . . .!' Mr Sparrow spluttered. 'Get it! Flip, grab it!'

The Hairy Thing giggled and sprang from table to

table, throwing anything it could lay its hands on. Ducking under a hail of bun-cases, Flip tried to catch it. In the swirl of sugary air, he could hardly see.

'Go,' Nick said.

The Hairy Thing stood on the draining-board, chewing. And saw Nick. It squealed and vanished.

Bim prodded Nick's ribs. 'What did you call it? It sounded like "brownie", but that's stupid.'

'I didn't mean that sort of brownie! It's like the water sprite.' Nick brushed the icing sugar out of his hair. 'This hasn't happened in Weston before. You must have done something really stupid.'

Mr Sparrow gazed at his topless cake. 'If we did do something, I wish we could undo it. Has Flippy told you about the dwarfs?'

Nick closed his eyes. 'Dwarfs as well. You should sell tickets.'

Mrs Sparrow started to mop up the mess. 'You know, Nicholas, it's strange. The Thing didn't like your grandma, either. She looked at it and it ran off. It must be something that runs in your family.'

'Well, a lot of things run in our family,' Nick said. 'I suppose people have told you we're all crazy. Or there's the one about Grandma dancing around a tree in the garden. She loves that one.'

'I think we'd better show you your room. And Nicholas . . .' Mrs Sparrow waited until he turned back. 'I'm very happy to have you here.'

Flip expected Nick to wince and shy away. Instead, the purple-black Weston eyes widened and a slow, slow smile spread over his face.

Bim scowled. 'Now I'll have to think of something else to call him. I can't call him "Wood Face" if he's going to smile like that.'

71

Nick raised his eyebrows at her. 'What about "Nick"?'

'Not if you keep calling me "Bong".'

'I thought you were called "Bong".'

'It's Bim!' She glared at him. 'Bim! I keep telling you it's Bim! It's always been Bim!'

Nick shrugged. 'OK, if that's what you want. But I think you look more like a "Bong" than a "Bim".'

Mrs Sparrow leading the way, they trouped upstairs. On the sxith step up, Flip remembered the hall mirror and swivelled to stare at it. The black letters said, 'Nicholas Weston. Welcome, Philip's best friend.'

No one spoke as Nick opened his bag and arranged his clothes along the blanket chest. Shoes, socks, shorts, shirt, everything in order, carefully folded and exactly the same distance apart.

'What're you doing?' Bim demanded. Nick ignored her so she dug her hand in her pocket and squeezed the Key. 'Nick, why've you put them all like that?'

'I daren't not do. I couldn't get dressed properly when I first came to Weston. I couldn't remember whether to put my socks on before my shoes. . .' Nick shivered and gave her a hard stare.

'I bet that was funny,' Bim said.

'I bet it wasn't.'

Mrs Sparrow pinched her arm. 'Bim, don't. I'm going to go downstairs and help your dad with the dinner. So all behave yourselves.'

When his mother had gone, Flip hurried to his room and brought the old book back. 'Nick, your grandma gave me this. I think you're supposed to write in it.'

'Oh, she brought it? I wondered.' Nick sat on the bed. 'All right, I'll do it, but I might make a mess of the spelling.'

'That's OK.'

'Flip, this is serious, you know.' Nick frowned until Flip stopped grinning. 'If I write this over to you, it means we're supposed to stay friends for the rest of our lives.'

Bim snorted. 'Don't put my name on it, then!'

'I wasn't going to,' Nick said and watched her stalk off.

Flip sighed. 'She really hates you. I suppose you could leave a space for her. In case you change your mind . . . Well, you never know.'

In the end, Flip nagged Nick into agreeing. Flip sat on the chest of drawers while Nick wrote on the old paper with a green felt-tip.

'How's this, Flip? "To Flip Sparrow. Take care of it for me."' Nick pulled a face. 'Then I've put this in brackets, "And Bim, as well, if she stops being such a pain." Signed, "Nick Weston, age thirteen".'

Flip nodded. 'That sounds about right. It might look better in blood, though. . .' And he wondered why Nick fell about laughing.

Mrs Sparrow had been meaning to check the shop's herb garden all week and Nick volunteered to help. He worked frighteningly hard, cutting the different herbs, arranging them on wooden trays and giving them paper labels. When she glanced over his shoulder, she saw that he had sketched the plant on each label. He had printed the names as well, 'paslee' for parsley, 'mind' for mint. When she corrected him, he seemed pleased.

Flip stretched out on the lawn and pretended not to be there. His dad had forgotten about him and Flip eavesdropped as his mum and dad talked.

'You're right, they're wonderful drawings.' Mr Sparrow rustled through the paper labels. 'Nick's a nice lad. Different, but nice. He sometimes looks at you and you'd think he knows everything in the world.'

'I think his grandma might be a witch,' Mrs Sparrow said.

Flip sat up.

'You mean hats and broomsticks?' Mr Sparrow managed a shaky laugh. 'That sort of witch?'

'I don't know.' Mrs Sparrow slid the box of herbs back into the wheelbarrow. 'David, this shop sells real magic. That man Cain was pure evil. And the other one, Typhoon or whatever he's called, turns into crocodiles and burns carpet . . .' She shivered, remembering the singed wallpaper and broken glass. 'Haven't you noticed Nick's eyes? They don't reflect the light and his grandma's are the same. I think that's what Nick meant about things running in his family. He meant magic things.'

Further down the garden, Nick drove Bim mad by doing one-handed cart-wheels. Every time she tried, she landed on her head. As Flip watched, Nick turned a perfect circle and stumbled into the wall.

'Are you all right?' Flip hurried over the grass. 'Nick?'

'I've tired myself out.' Nick scrubbed his grazed elbow. 'I should go to bed and sleep it off or I'll feel terrible tomorrow.'

'We haven't even had supper yet . . . But I think you're right.' Flip shook his head. 'You look really awful.'

'Thanks!'

Flip steered him through the house. 'Anyone would think you're drunk, the way you're walking. Can you manage the stairs?'

'I'll have to, won't I?'

74

'I could carry you,' Flip said and Nick grinned. 'All right, maybe I couldn't. I'll just walk behind you in case you get dizzy.'

They staggered into Nick's room. Some time during the evening, Nick had hung his stone-with-a-hole over one bed post. Flip decided not to ask what it was for. He watched Nick fumble into his pyjamas.

'Do you want the light leaving on?'

Nick glared at him. 'What for? You'll be asking me if I want a glass of milk and a biscuit, in a minute.'

'You can have a glass of milk if you want, Nick.' Flip ducked but the scrunched-up sock still hit him on the nose. 'How about a cocoa?'

'Get out of here, Sparrow!' Nick stuffed the sock into his washing bag.

'I just want to make sure you're all right.' Flip caught the washing bag and threw it back, tried not to look impressed when Nick headed it, and caught it, again. 'Where do you want this?'

'Hang it on the bottom of the bed. I'll wake up thinking it's Christmas.' Nick crawled into bed and tugged the sheet up to his chin. 'I'm going to sleep now. So push off.' And his eyes slid shut.

'But Nick . . . Nick? You can't be asleep, just like that . . .!'

Nick's body curled like a baby rabbit, face buried in his folded arms. No doubt about it, he was fast asleep. Flip shook his head, turned the light off and tiptoed out of the room.

Ice-cream and Bicycles

Nick woke with a huge yawn, stretched and gazed at a ceiling that had changed colour overnight. Why was it pale blue? He sat up. The bed was in the wrong place. And the window. Outside, the sea breeze strengthened towards a wind storm. Then he remembered the pattern on the curtains. Flip's house! Of course, he was staying at the shop for a few weeks. Stupid to forget that. Nick stretched again, and padded towards his clothes. He trod on something soft. It was his shirt.

The brownie had been busy. One sock swung from the curtain-rail, another lurked under the table. Nick's shorts dangled from the lampshade and his lucky stone had vanished. The room spun around him as he tried desperately not to panic. But everything had gone. He could not find anything and he could not remember how to look.

The kitchen door opened without bothering to turn its handle and a pale, trembling figure slid inside. Four Sparrow faces stared.

'I can't find my shoes.'

Flip dropped his spoon. 'Nick, what's wrong? You're dead white!'

'It moved my things.' Nick shivered. 'I can't find my shoes.'

76

He swayed in the doorway, barefoot with his shirt unbuttoned because his fingers had forgotten how to fasten buttons. Mrs Sparrow almost stood up but Bim beat her to it.

'Honestly, Nick, you are stupid. Come on, I'll help you.'

'I don't want you to help me!'

Bim grinned and dragged him back into the hall. 'I know.'

Mr Sparrow drank some tea. 'Bim's a little monster, sometimes. But that might be exactly the way to deal with this.'

When Bim and Nick came back, Flip knew that his dad was right. Whatever they had said to each other, Bim did not hate Nick any more.

'Well,' Mr Sparrow smiled with relief. 'And who wants toast?'

He pushed the button. Springs twanged. Two pieces of toast whizzed out of the toaster like guided missiles and shattered the plaster on the kitchen ceiling. In the oven, the brownie giggled and spluttered.

'That's it.' Nick hauled his shirt over his head. 'Come here!' He yanked the oven door open and seized a hairy arm. 'Now, take this and push off!'

The brownie squawked with excitement and snatched Nick's shirt, pulling it on back-to-front. Then it vanished under the kitchen door.

Flip realized that he had dropped his cornflakes on his knee. 'How did you do that?'

'That's how you get rid of brownies. Give them some clothes and they go.' Nick shrugged. 'I thought a Sparrow would know that.'

After breakfast, Flip and Bim showed Nick around the shop, tried to tell him where everything was and gave up because he always knew. When Bim tried to impress him with the crystal ball, he juggled it around the room until she cried with laughter. Nick almost laughed as well, but something made him gaze into the cool crystal. Under his fingers, grey mist coiled into a face with a shark's smile.

The sequin sprinkle of light came first, sliding under the door like cold water. It lit Nick's face, but not his dark eyes. The bell over the shop door rang and Solomon Cain strolled inside, one hand raised to straighten his wind-tossed hair. Seeing Nick there, he let the door slam back into the wall.

'Every time I come here, some Weston gets in my way.' Cain's shark teeth glittered. 'It's starting to make me very angry. I didn't realize you were staying here, Nicholas.'

Nick stiffened. 'I've never met you. Don't call me Nicholas.'

'I'll call you anything I like. No, you've never met me. But you know what I am, don't you?' Cain's smile twisted. 'You've got the Weston eyes. Everything they see sinks into them and nothing ever escapes. And you know things no one's ever told you.'

'What I don't need is another wizard.' Nick rested his elbows on the counter and waited for Cain's first move. 'If you're after the Key, you might as well forget it.'

Flip nodded. 'It isn't for sale.' Then he flinched as Cain's eyes pinned him.

'Then I'll have to steal it, won't I?' Cain spread his left hand and slid the gold ring into his palm. 'Watch! It can be as small as a pin . . .' The ring shrank to a gold spot against his thumb. '. . . or large enough to squeeze around a boy's neck.'

Spinning gold looped through the air and Nick

shoved Flip sideways, punching the ring through the shop door. Cain clicked his fingers and the ring boomeranged back, hissing and dodging Nick's fists. It wanted Flip's neck. It wanted to strangle him.

Mrs Sparrow had been in the garden, chasing the washing. When she heard Bim scream and opened the kitchen door, there was a clear channel of air from the back garden to the front pavement. With a mad squeal, the wind crashed past her, throwing her face-down on the kitchen floor. It tore along the hall and into the shop. In the centre of the hurricane, a bright blue door dazzled sun-bright, dragging its trail of darkness and crackling power.

'Great!' Nick clung to the shop counter for dear life. 'Just great! You've only opened the Door to the Other, Flip!'

Two jets of darkness ripped through the Door and tossed Cain on to the hall carpet. Half the shop flew into the street, herbs tearing free of the rafters, packs of cards splitting and fluttering into the gutters. The crystal ball shattered against the curb. A final spat of temper and the wind swept the blue door on to Caliburn Hill.

Broken pottery scrunched as Flip stood up. Wind-bruised, ginger fringe in his eyes, he inhaled a nose-full of shredded herbs and sneezed. 'Did you see that?!'

'Everyone saw that!' Nick yelled. 'I told you, it's the Door to the Other. Come on, there isn't time to stand with your face hanging out. Run!' He leapt through the shop door and ran.

Maxie had been washing the salon window while Devon sat on the doorstep, tightening things on his bike. Then a hurricane had blown out of the Sparrows' shop.

'Bim, what's happening?'

Bim grabbed her arm. 'We've got to follow that Door.'

'Bim, I'm cleaning the windows!'

'Oh, Maxie . . . Come on!'

Devon yelled as Flip jumped over him and nicked his bike.

'Sorry, Dev. I need it to chase the Door.' Flip swung into the saddle. 'Thanks . . .'

The Door travelled with the gale, following the busy street towards the Promenade. Wispy darkness streamed behind it in twin comets' tails.

For the second time in three days, Flip chased something weird that had escaped from the shop, not sure what he was going to do if he caught it, just knowing that he had to follow it. This time, Nick sprinted in front of him, next to him, behind him as Devon's bike sped down the hill.

Mr Crouch the ice-cream man had left the pier for his daily trip around Weston. A dozen wind-swept people waited while he scraped ice-cream into antique cones. He dug the scoop into the mass of vanilla ice cream, pulled and swore. The scoop refused to budge. He put his back into it, jerking at the scoop handle. It still refused to budge. He rammed a foot against the counter and the scoop twisted, snapped out of his grip, and sank into the ice-cream.

'Flippin' 'eck! Now where's that gone? Come 'ere . . .'

As he leaned into the deep tub of ice-cream, a pale, vanilla hand reached upwards, followed by a vanilla arm. Ice-cream fingers closed around his neck and pulled. The queue of people screamed as Mr Crouch disappeared, head-first, into his own ice-cream.

80

'Look at that!' Maxie pointed to the two legs kicking out of the ice-cream van window. 'It's Mr Crouch.'

Muffled yells echoed from the ice-cream tub. 'Gerroff! Gettitoffomeee!! 'Elp!!'

The hot wash-leather still steamed in Maxie's hand. She gripped the van window and sprang onto the counter. Just below her, the vanilla fingers clenched on Mr Crouch's collar. Maxie wrapped the hot leather around them and they twisted and melted, slithering back into the tub.

'Come on, Max!' Bim yelled. 'Come on, we're losing it!'

The door had reached the corner, its next stop the main road.

'Help! Someone . . . Help!'

Nick stopped running. A large lady in slippers hobbled towards him, closely followed by a vacuum cleaner. The cleaner's plug thrashed behind it on its flex, sparking off the wall and into the road and back. Its long suction tube snaked forwards and its nozzle opened and closed like a plastic piranha-mouth. As Nick watched, it pounced and bit a hole in the lady's dress.

Nick threw himself on top of the cleaner and wrestled it down. It struggled to break free and vacuumed him, painfully. Snake-strong tubing whipped tight around his neck and the plug cracked his shin. The tube twisted and suddenly Nick fought for breath. Tears in his eyes, he fumbled along the plastic case for the off switch. Couldn't see it. Couldn't feel it. The vacuum groaned and hummed, tightening its tube until no blood or air could squeeze under it. Nick's fingertips shivered with pins and needles and black patches danced in his eyes. He

81

was being strangled. Choking, he wriggled over the cleaner's hard wheels and his thumb found the switch. Stabbed it with all of his strength. The vacuum cleaner slumped onto the pavement, dead.

'Are you all right?' Flip had heard the woman screaming and pedalled back. He gawked in disbelief. 'What are you grinning at? This is terrible!' But he had never seen Nick look happier.

'I haven't had so much fun . . . in years.' Nick gasped. 'The Door's letting things out. . . From the Other.'

'What Other? What's happening?' Flip balanced on the bike, torn between pedalling after the Door and finding out what Nick meant. 'Nick, what Other . . .? Oi!'

Bicycle pedals squirmed and creaked into two metal hands. They snapped shut around Flip's feet and gave a metal giggle before starting to pedal backwards. Down the hill.

Nick leapt up. 'Flip! Jump off!'

'I can't! It won't let me . . . Nick, help!' Horrified, Flip tried the brakes but the bicycle ignored him. 'Nick . . .! Bim!'

The pedals moved faster, backwards, not caring whether any cars were coming or how much their rider tried to stop them. They wound their silvery fingers around Flip's feet and pedalled for dear life.

As the bike accelerated, Flip twisted the handle-bars and kicked downwards. And again, heaving the handle-bars from side to side, jamming the brakes. The bicycle decided that enough was enough, bucked its back wheels and threw him in a leggy cartwheel on to the grass verge. Two metal hands gripped his feet, angrily, as the bicycle sped away.

'Owww! Nick, help!' Flip attacked the metal fingers

with his own bony ones. 'They're breaking my feet!'

Flip and Nick took a pedal hand each and fought to prize the fingers open. Silvery knuckles groaned but tightened their grip.

'They're like mouse-traps! I can't . . . shift . . . them . . .' Flip dug under the metal fingers and jerked them upwards. The hand flew into the air and snapped shut on his nose. 'Oww!! By dose! Ged id off by dose!'

The second hand caught Nick's ankle, twisted and slammed him flat on his back.

'Oww! Baxie . . . Bib . . . Cub ad help us!' Tears streamed down Flip's face. 'Do subthig! Adythig!'

Maxie held Flip's head by the ears while Bim tugged the metal hand. The harder she tugged, the harder the hand gripped Flip's poor nose.

"Sno good, Flippy,' Bim said. 'We'll have to cut it off.'

'You're dod cutting by dose off!' Flip screamed.

'The hand off, not your nose!'

'I cad't wait that log.' Flip scuttled to Nick's side and ducked his head until the metal hands touched. 'Ged theb off, together . . . Od, two, three. . .!'

A double twist and the hands clanged shut, fingers scrunching fingers. They crumpled into a solid lump of metal.

Eyes squeezed shut, Flip stroked the throbbing, red blob that was his nose. Beside him on the grass, Nick rubbed his grazed ankle. Maxie wiped ice-cream stains from her knees. The Door had vanished.

'It could have blown out of sight or it could have got stuck somewhere.' Nick said. 'You can only see it when it's moving.'

'Brilliant!' Bim glared at him. 'How can we find it if we can't see it?'

'It's not my fault. That's just the way it is.' Nick stood up and tested his ankle. 'I think I'm in one piece. How about you, Flip?'

Flip carefully let go of his nose. When it did not fall off, he managed a crooked grin. 'So far so good. I just wish . . .'

'That's him!' Maxie gasped. 'That's the man who turns into crocodiles. . . !'

The black car skidded into the opposite pavement and Qabahl leapt out, face wild with hatred. The black stick glinted in his fist.

'Run!' Nick dragged Flip on to his feet. 'Flip, get out of here. I'll try to slow him down . . .'

'No way!' Flip shook him off. 'Look, there's people everywhere. He won't try anything with people watching.'

'Of course he will . . .!' Nick bit his lip helplessly. 'Flip, you don't know how powerful he is. He'll just stop the people watching.'

The stick whistled and Nick's shirt-sleeve sliced through as if a razor had slashed it. It came too close to Maxie. She snatched the stick and broke it in half, throwing the pieces on to the road.

'Maxie!' Nick stared at her. 'Don't . . . He'll hurt you.'

'I don't care!' But she shivered, watching the fragments of wood turn to sand.

The sand whipped past their feet, sizzled and cracked and was the black stick again. The silver point hovered, waiting to draw more blood. Then suddenly the air chilled.

Bim shivered. 'It's the other one. It's not fair. . .'

For the first time in eleven years, the two magicians came face to face. Cain's ice-cold evil shimmered in circles of light while Qabahl's black fire and animal strength snarled back at him. Neither spoke.

Cain's ring stretched to a huge circle, clanging on to the street. It surrounded the four friends and the two enemies. Nothing outside could move, nothing inside could escape.

Flip gaped as balls of fire bounced off rings of light, blinding flashes crashed against veils of sand. A rain of rings fell, lassooing Qabahl's arms. They snapped shut and he screamed, thrashing free in a gush of black smoke. When the smoke cleared, his body had changed. The crocodile's red-hot eyes burned from a face horribly stretched, pointed, crocodile-snouted. His bottom teeth curled over his top lip and his jagged bones strained against his skin, as if an animal skeleton lived in a man's body. He screamed curses so horrible that Nick staggered away.

'Don't listen!' Nick gasped. 'Don't listen!'

Now Cain started to change. His plump body paled and took on a glassy shine, his eyes almost dead-fish white, empty as rattles. The pavement frosted under his feet and the drains froze all down the hill.

Spells held the people outside the ring statue-stiff with drooping mouths and crossed eyes. Before the magicians could guess what he was doing, Nick prized grass and soil out of the verge and crushed it onto the gold. The earth broke the circle and the people snapped back to life.

'Now run!' Nick grabbed Maxie and Bim. 'Run!'

Behind him, Cain's fist clipped Flip on the nose. Flip yelped and ran.

'They daren't let so many people see them do magic,' Nick said. 'If it got in the papers, the place would be swarming with PPs. And some are good enough to give them real problems.'

'PPs? What are PPs—oh no!'

'Devon's bike!' Flip remembered the bike in a rush of blood to the nose. 'What am I going to say?'

'If I was you, Flip, I wouldn't say anything! Just keep out of Devon's way for a few years.'

'Oh fantastic! I wish I knew what was going on.' Flip glanced at Nick. 'I wish certain people would tell me. Hey, the dark's gone.' Above their heads, the shop roof glowed in the sun. 'Even if you won't tell us everything, Nick, why's the dark gone? Come on, it's only fair.'

'Why've I got to be fair? I don't want to be fair . . .' Nick glared at the pleading faces. 'All right, it's gone because the Door's gone. The dark's the evil leaking from the Other Side. And now the Door's floating around Weston letting Things out every time the wind blows.'

Flip gulped. 'What sort of things?'

Nick smiled, nastily. 'You don't want to know.'

Mrs Sparrow had waited for them at the shop door. Pale with worry, she gave each of them a hug and a kiss. Behind her, the shop hid under a layer of ruined herbs and crushed pottery.

'You'd better see the cellar,' she said. 'It's getting worse.'

Numb, Flip watched two dozen dwarfs disappear into a tunnel the size of the London Underground. Pit-props and railway tracks covered the floor. Flip wished that the Key could make Nick talk without him noticing. Not much else would. Nick liked to keep his secrets.

The friends ate a picnic lunch in the Sparrows' garden and Flip's nose slowly shrank back to its normal size. It itched like crazy.

'We've got to find the Door.' Flip chomped his stick of celery and drank the juice. 'And it might help if we knew what it was. And what the Key did. And what PPs are . . . Nick, come on! You've got to tell us!'

Nick shook his head. 'It'd take too long. As long as the Door's letting things out, something really bad could happen.'

Flip thought about that. 'OK, we'll get going in a minute. But I'm not moving until you tell me what the PPs are. You said they could give Typhoon real trouble so why don't you get them to help us?'

'Because . . .!' Three pairs of eyes waited and Nick flinched. 'It isn't easy any more. Until you came, I knew I hadn't got to tell anyone anything. Now you all know bits and pieces. I don't know what to say.'

Maxie smiled at him. 'We won't tell anyone else, Nick. We can all keep secrets, can't we?'

Flip nodded. Then Bim, reluctantly.

'OK.' Nick started to pace the grass. 'It's not much good calling the police for people like Cain, so the magic world set up the Psychic Police. They're all magicians and we call them the PP's. They'd come running if they knew what Cain and Qabahl were up to.'

'Why don't you tell them, then?' Flip asked. 'We could do with some help.'

Nick stopped pacing. 'I can't tell them, Flip. It's your fault the Door's blown away. If the PPs find out, they could make your mum and dad leave the shop. They might say the Sparrows aren't fit to keep it any more.' He bit his lip. 'I'm sorry, Flip, but I told you not to mess about with magic.'

'Thanks for telling us, anyway.' Flip swallowed a lump in his throat. 'We'd better get after the Door.'

Maxie frowned. 'All I can think of is following the wind . . . But how do you follow the wind?'

Bim shrugged. 'Weather forecast, I suppose.'

'The radio,' Nick said. 'Turn the radio on.'

'What . . .?'

'Flip, turn the radio on. I just know . . .' Nick shook himself and shivered. 'Please, just turn the radio on.'

And the radio news announced that a freak storm had blown into the amusement park an hour ago . . .

Nick nodded. 'That's where it is. At the fun fair.'

When they told Mrs Sparrow where they were going, she sighed. 'I've got a feeling that some of this is your fault, Flip, so you've got to put it right. Promise me you'll be careful.'

They promised and she gave them some change, in case they had to ride any of the amusements. Bim filled her pockets with salt and vinegar crisps and Flip filled his with twisted pieces of paper and as much magic as he could carry. He decided not to mention it to Nick, just in case . . .

A last wave to Mrs Sparrow and they ran down the road, catching the first bus along the Prom.

'It could be anywhere.' Maxie stared between the fairground rides. 'This is going to be really hard.'

'It might be stuck in one of the rides,' Bim said. 'We might have to try all of them.'

Flip groaned. 'You would say that! Still, I don't suppose it'll matter if we do try a ride or two. I fancy the big wheel.'

'I fancy the ghost train.' Bim pulled a ghostly face. 'I like to hear everyone scream.'

'You would.' Nick gazed up to the top seats of the big wheel. 'I don't know, it's very high.'

'Well, what do you like?' Flip asked. 'Dodgems? Speedway?'

No breeze ruffled Nick's hair or rattled Maxie's beads. The door would be invisible. People on the helter skelter decided that the way down was longer than they had thought. They seemed to be sliding forever and getting nowhere. A pale green shape drifted towards the ghost train.

Maxie smiled. 'I like the ghost train as well.'

'That's it, then.' Bim grabbed Maxie's hand. 'Let's go.'

A giant, painted skull swallowed the cars into the ghost-train shed and horrible shrieks leaked from its mouth. Bim and Maxie's car jolted forwards first. The ticket man waited for two minutes to give them time to move around the track, then pressed a button.

'There's never enough room for my legs in these things,' Flip grumbled, then oofed as the car bounced ahead. 'I bet you scream, Nick.'

'I bet I don't.'

The car plunged into the warm darkness and their eyes opened wide, trying to see. A green skeleton lunged at them, rattling fluorescent bones. Recorded screams crackled from the ancient speakers.

'Pathetic,' Nick muttered. 'I could do better.'

He gave a blood-chilling shriek that sent Flip yelping into the side of the car.

'Nick! Don't. . .'

'Well, you said I'd scream.' Cobwebs tickled their faces. 'Yuk!'

The track snaked in tight coils, bursting through black swing doors into different horror scenes. The shed was quite small but the rails doubled back on themselves again and again, making the place seem huge. Through another door, painted with vampire teeth. Dracula rose from his coffin and plastic bats fluttered overhead.

'Pathetic!'

Another real-life howl echoed through the darkness.

'Stop it, Nick!'

'Wasn't me.'

Flip squinted towards Nick's voice. 'Oh, come on!'

'It wasn't me.'

The howl echoed again, closer. Flip recognized it and his stomach heaved. 'It's him! Nick, it's Typhoon! He's in here. Oh no, he's in here with us!'

Ghosts

Another howl rocked the air above them and a strange shouted word rang in their ears.

'It's a Word of Power . . . Egyptian. . .' Nick whispered.

The car jerked to a halt, suddenly silent in the darkness.

'I think he'll frighten us first.' Nick swallowed and sat further back in the metal seat. 'He likes frightening people.'

'What are you going to do?' Flip touched Nick's arm and felt the muscles quiver. 'Nick . . .?'

'I don't know.'

Qabahl roared into the car, screaming. His elbow bruised Flip's neck and his bony fingers crushed Flip's shoulder. Lifted. Flip kicked, desperately. No use. The fingers were iron pincers breaking his shoulder. They tossed Flip away as if he were a dry twig. A second of falling in pitch blackness, not knowing if he was going to smash his face on the track, and Flip crashed on to the concrete. His head cracked on a rail and he felt sick and his arms were dead, no strength in them at all.

A green glow spread through the blackness. On hands and knees, Flip groped into Dracula's coffin.

He glimpsed the outline of the car and Nick half-way out, straining to break free. Qabahl held him by the shirt. He played Nick like a fish, letting him almost fall over the edge, then dragging him back. The bruises on Nick's face shone grey on white.

'And I'll take this pretty bracelet for a start.' Qabahl ripped the copper band from Nick's wrist, dug it in, took Nick's skin with it.

'Leave him alone!' Flip yelled. 'Leave him alone!'

'Give me the Key first. One of you's got it.' Qabahl showed his crocodile teeth. 'And I'll find out which . . . One way or another.'

'You wouldn't let him go if I did!' Flip had to keep the man talking. Someone was bound to realize that the train had stopped. 'What do you want the Key for?'

'For what it could get me.' Qabahl's voice hissed with greed. 'I could get everything I'd ever wanted . . . Your grandmother'll wish she never met me, Weston. I told her she'd be sorry.'

The green glow floated past the coffin, past the plastic bats on their pieces of wire. The ghost-train car turned apple green, then Qabahl's face. And then Flip managed to squawk with pure shock.

'There's a ghost behind you,' Nick said.

Qabahl snorted. 'Very funny!'

'Oh, I don't think so. It looks very angry.'

Qabahl sneered into Nick's eyes but they did not reflect the green, throbbing ghost. 'Can't you do better than that? Do you think I'd run off screaming from a ghost?'

The ghost gazed at Qabahl's neck thoughtfully, unrolled several metres of iron chain and shook them under the man's sneering nose. It worked every time. Qabahl spun on his seat and Nick squirmed free, nosediving for the floor. With a frantic rip of paper, Flip hurled his packet of Fixit Dust. Electricity sparked into the car's engine and it shot forwards, taking Qabahl with it. A happy ghost perched on Qabahl's shoulders, one hand plucking the man's hair out, one hand twisting chains around his neck, one hand tweaking the man's long nose.

Flip hauled Nick upright. 'Let's get out of here!'

Black curtains opened on a man with striped braces over his vest. 'What the flippin 'eck's going on? Ruddy kids! It says "Keep in the Cars".' He grabbed Nick and Flip by their collars. 'Can't you read?'

Flip met Nick's slow smile and smiled back. Nick could have said, "No, I can't read". Neither of them said anything as the man bundled them through the fire exit and into the sunshine.

'What happened to you two?' Bim said. 'We've been out for. . . . Nick, you're all bruised. Flip, you're all dusty. What happened?'

'Typhoon happened,' Flip said. 'He's in there with a green ghost. Let's get lost before he comes out. I don't want him following us home.'

They ran past the helter-skelter. The spiral slide spun upwards at the same speed as the mats spun downwards. Several boys had circled the tower for ten minutes and their faces glistened sick yellow.

'Flip, where are we going?' Maxie panted beside him, beads flying. 'The Hob's a dead end. We'd be trapped if we went on it.'

'It's your town. Where can we hide?' For two minutes, Flip had almost forgotten Nick. Now he glanced back. 'Nick, you're shaking . . .'

'I know. He hurt me . . .' Nick held his ribs and took two shuddery breaths. 'We can hide in the Hob

Café. It closed when someone got food-poisoning. Qabahl'll send his things but I think I can fool them.'

Flip winced. 'What sort of things . . .?'

Inside the old café, Flip hugged knees to chest and tried not to think too hard. Square holes in the floor showed where tables had been ripped free and rough planks blocked the windows. Flip inhaled dust and Bim's feet smell and the new-washed cotton of Nick's shirt.

Nick rubbed his skinned wrist. 'Grandma gave me that bracelet and Qabahl knew . . . That lousy thief!' His lips trembled and he bit them to hold them still. 'I hate him, Flip. He hates me and I hate him back.'

'Maybe he won't look in here,' Bim said. 'You can't see we've got in because we used the Key. All the locks and boards are still up . . .'

'But he knows we've got the Key.' Nick shook his head. 'No, he'll look, all right. He'll look everywhere.'

Sunlight edged the door and slitted between the boards of the window. Flip had read his watch three times when the light at the bottom of the door vanished. A line of black fire ran along the wood, spat and hissed to nothing. Then the sand started to blow inside. Trickles melted to rivers to a carpet of sand drifting onto the battered floor.

'It needs eyes to see and legs to move,' Nick said. 'Quick, tie your jeans bottoms up! Use your laces! Then cross your fingers. I'll do the talking. Sit still, keep your fingers crossed, and don't panic.'

A ripple spread over the sand, quivered and vanished. Ten seconds. Twenty . . . Another ripple heaved and split into smaller ripples, which split again, making sandy worms on the wood. The worms fidgeted and looked a bit lost, for a minute. Then every worm snapped over on itself, hardening into a shell. The shells curled into a tail at one end, legs in the middle. Legs with sharp points. The curled tail twisted and suddenly the sand shapes were scorpions. Scorpions with poisoned tails.

When Nick spoke, his voice was a whisper. 'You can't see us, can't hear us, can't feel us, can't smell us, can't taste us. You're sand and sand can't see or hear or smell or feel or taste. You can't. You can't.'

Squads of spiny-footed scorpions marched out of the sand. They covered every millimetre of floor, wall and ceiling. Maxie closed her eyes as three scorpions scuttled over her legs. They tickled and she wanted to bat them away.

Bim glared at the horrible things. If Nick had not told her to sit still, she would have stamped on them. When one crawled over her face, she glared at it and only closed her eye when its feet touched her lashes.

Flip decided that scorpions were his least favourite insect. If they were an insect. Were they an insect? It seemed very important to know. Then a fat scorpion fell inside his shirt. He would have gone into orbit but Nick pinched his arm.

'If it gets stuck, it'll just turn back to sand, Flip. Don't worry, it won't sting. It doesn't know you're there.' Nick closed his eyes as scorpions crawled over them, through his hair and on to the wall.

Flip's nose itched badly. The bruises must be healing inside. He wanted to sneeze and the thing in his shirt disintegrated and tickled its way down his ribs. He wanted to yell 'YYYUUUKKK!!!' at the top of his voice and jump up and down and tear his shirt off to get the sand out.

The scorpions gathered on the ceiling, pushing

and shoving. Tails tangled, pincers locked. . .

'Close your eyes, they're going to fall!' Nick yelled. Sand rained down. 'Now, up and shake!' Nick leapt around the floor as if it were red hot. 'Get the sand out of your clothes. Come on, Flip!'

If Qabahl had been standing outside the door, he would have heard them. The café bounced with leaping feet. Flip yanked his shirt free and scrubbed his chest, Maxie put her head between her knees and rattled her beads until she was dizzy. Bim looked like a clown, red curls all on end.

'Now freeze!'

No one moved. The sand waited for a moment, rippled, formed a thick mat and slid back under the door.

Mrs Weston listened to her grandson's calm voice at the other end of the telephone and all of her worst fears seemed to be coming true. 'Nicholas, are you sure you're all right? Qabahl didn't hurt you?'

'I'm just a bit bruised. But things are going crazy.' Nick hesitated, then ploughed on. 'Grandma, Flip's opened the Door to the Other. He's got the Key and Qabahl and Cain are both after it. Can we come to the Castle? They might try to follow us . . .'

'Nicholas, of course come here! Straight away!' Her voice shook and she took a deep breath. 'I had no idea that you knew about things like that. We have to talk, Nicholas.'

'I know, Grandma.'

Flip rested against one of the pier's legs and got his breath back. The fastest way to the castle was straight along the beach and up the cliff path. But from here on, they were alone. The cliff's shadow blocked the sun and the air was too cold for sun-worshippers. No one wanted to speak any more. When Nick ran for the dark bulk of the cliff, his friends followed in silence. Behind them, stick-eyes boggling, the small crab scuttled sideways, squirmed and changed into a footprint, racing over the beach to find its master.

Nick knew the cliff better than anywhere in Weston but he had to look at his grazed wrist twice to remember which way was left. Damp air turned the grass into a soggy tangle and the path squelched under his trainers. When he glanced over his shoulder, he saw the wall of fog that had appeared from nowhere. Cold fog on a mild day.

'He's here,' Nick said.

The fog swirled between their legs and a thick layer of cloud slid over the sky. The last, rosy light drained from the cliff top.

'It's like a giant dimmer switch,' Flip whispered.

Nick stumbled and dug both fists into the grass. Dark, crooked arms of trees pushed out of the mist and long grass trapped his shins.

'I can see the castle lights!' Flip squeezed forwards. 'I'll take over, Nick. Watch our backs.'

Where was the lawn? They should have reached the lawn by now. Instead, they tripped over sharp rocks. A dark shape loomed above Flip's head, twisted arms clawing towards his face. And they were real arms.

'Look out!' Flip dived and Qabahl's nails scraped his neck. 'Split up! Everyone split up!'

One second and the four friends had scattered into the mist.

The fog shuffled noises, tossed them in all directions, made the sea seem to come from everywhere. Flip knew that Qabahl pounded after him. The man's feet scrambled over stones, thudded on the turf between, gaining every step. A jump and a slither and Flip crashed through a hedge on to freshly dug soil. And collided with a body. He fell flat.

'Flip, it's me!' Maxie hauled him up. 'It's me!'

'Max, he's right behind us . . . The Key!' Flip groaned and dragged it out of his pocket. 'OPEN!!'

The fog split as if a knife had carved it, sky to earth. As clear as a torch-beam, it swept the grass, crossed fruit trees, herb garden, gravel drive. And found the castle's patched stone.

'Run, Max!'

The mist closed behind them, leaving Qabahl lost in his own fog.

Flip's mind raced as fast as his legs. The Key opened the castle door and he was inside. What he wanted was a weapon to use against Qabahl and that meant it had to be a magic weapon.

'Fixit Dust, Max!' Flip grinned at Maxie's blank face. 'I'm going to fix the weather machine and blow Typhoon right off the cliff!'

They ran up the spiral stairs. Sweat stung Flip's eyes and he blinked and used the Key and slid across the tower to the weather machine.

'Max, help me get it to the window.' Flip grappled the box of magnets, umbrella spokes sticking in his ear. 'What did Nick say . . .?'

'It needs sun on its wings,' Maxie said. 'But there's no sun.'

'There will be.'

The Key opened the window, then the clouds. Red light sparked along the umbrella spokes, over the tin cans studding the two wings.

'Stand back.' Flip struggled up the high, front wheel on to the box of magnets.

'Flip, you don't know how it works . . .'

'All you can do is pedal it, Max.' Flip wriggled his toes on to the pedals. 'Just stand right back.'

Teeth gritted, Flip pedalled. Tin cans clattered, bicycle wheels spun, umbrella spokes twanged and pinged. Flip pedalled harder and Maxie squawked as pure energy flashed through the window.

'Flip!' Maxie sneezed and coughed. 'Flip! Are you all right?'

Flip's head appeared, covered in dust. Two metres above it, a cloud the size of a small handbag hovered and turned a miserable grey.

Flip winced upwards. 'Oh brilliant!'

The cloud looked even more miserable and started to rain on to Flip's face.

'Maybe you have to tell it what you want?' Maxie touched the bicycle seat gingerly. 'We'd like some wind, please. I don't think there's enough sun, Flip. It's trying, but it isn't strong enough.'

Flip was angry and frustrated, so the cloud was angry and frustrated. It blackened and thundered.

'And you shut up!' Flip yelled, and ducked a flash of lightning. 'Hey! Hey, stop it!'

The more Flip yelled, the more the cloud threw lightning. A white corkscrew of electricity hit the weather machine, sparked through it, spun its bicycle wheels. Cold wind gushed through the castle window.

'It works!' Flip yelled. 'Max, point the umbrella. Try to blow the fog away. I'm going out . . .' He grinned at the happy white cloud. 'I've had an idea.'

Nick heard the waves crash on the rocks below Weston Point. He had run as fast as he could run and fallen on to sharp rocks and stayed down.

Breathing hurt. He slid on to his knees and saw the lights again. He almost cried with relief. They just had to be the castle lights. As he stumbled forwards, he prayed that the waves were not really so loud. Every step seemed to take him closer to the sea.

The lights vanished. Stunned, Nick tried to understand, then knew. Qabahl had been playing with him again. Now he was really lost. Two shaky steps forward and he bumped into a wooden sign. It might be telling him to go straight ahead or it might be warning him not to. In the dim light, he could not make the letters spell a single word.

'Nick! Don't move!' Bim squealed. 'Don't move!'

'Shut up! He'll hear . . .'

'Nick, you're on the edge. Don't move.'

Nick froze, arms clutching at the fog, feeling nothing. When a hand closed on his shirt, he panicked and ran forwards. Bim kicked the back of his knee and he sat, feet scraping over the grassy edge. Stones spattered, bouncing on rock and falling into the giant waves. The empty air surged with salt-spray all the way down to St Brigid's Rock.

'Stupid!' Bim slid next to him. 'I told you not to move!'

'Well, well. So there you are.'

The stink of burning meat caught in their throats. Red-hot crocodile eyes burned out of the fog. Bim had not seen Qabahl as the crocodile. She squawked and slithered into Nick's elbow. Mist swirled and the crocodile shivered back into Qabahl's white face, his animal sneer.

'Get up.'

Nick stood. 'Run, Bim. I'll keep him away from you.'

Bim tried to see his face. The first breath of a breeze

came from the castle and tickled through her hair.

'I'm not leaving you,' she said.

'Don't be a twit! Run!'

'No.' Bim stuck her bottom lip out. 'I'm not leaving you. And it's no good yelling . . . What's that?'

Fluttering. Swooping. Nick twisted as the big bird shrieked out of the mist. 'Sorath! Sorath, take him!'

Qabahl twisted as well, ready with his sand magic and black flame. Nick threw himself into the man's legs. Off balance, Qabahl staggered on to the loose rocks at the cliff edge.

A noise clattered down the cliff path. At first Bim thought she was hearing things. It sounded like a heavy shower of rain and distant thunder, on two legs. And was that a flash of very small lightning?

Stronger and stronger breezes buffetted the fog. Bim glimpsed trees, then the witch-hat towers of the castle. And then her brother, pounding towards her under a small black cloud.

'Oh no,' Nick groaned. 'I told him not to mess about with magic.'

Flip worked on anger. He had to be furious, angry enough to make the cloud's little spats of lightning dangerous. One look at Bim's grazed knuckles and the anger bubbled over. A gust of air lifted the last of the fog away and Qabahl reared up, a dark figure with clenched fists silhouetted against the red sky. The cloud swelled with Flip's anger, growing to double its size, double again. A deafening roll of thunder knocked Flip flat and lightning shattered the cliff at Qabahl's feet.

'Now, Maxie!' Flip waved at the castle. 'Now!'

Staggering, the cliff crumbling under his feet, Qabahl saw the tree-tops bend, heard the squeal of wind. A great wall of air struck him in the chest. At

101

the same time, Nick leapt for his bulging jacket pocket and ripped it open. Like a bottomless pit, it showered the ground with stolen watches, purses, jewellery, a copper bracelet, season tickets for the London Tube . . . Qabahl screamed and fell towards St Brigid's Rock.

Nick watched, clutching the copper bracelet to his ribs. Qabahl's shrieking body thickened, grew armoured scales and a thrashing tail. It squirmed into a rigid ball of crocodile-flesh and hit the rock and bounced, rolling along the edge of the cliff and into the water. A last roar at the cliff and the crocodile dived, swimming towards Weston Bay.

'We beat him,' Nick said. 'We didn't give him time to use his magic.' He slid the copper bracelet back on to his wrist. 'As long as he thinks we're just stupid kids, he's going to give us the chance to fool him . . . Cain!'

'What?' Flip wheeled around but there was no Cain. 'Nick, I nearly died! What about Cain?'

'Where is he?' Nick swung his arms over the view of Weston lights and the dark crescent of the sea. 'Why didn't Cain come after us as well?'

'Hey, one magician's enough! I'm just glad he didn't.' Flip shuddered at the thought. 'Come on, Maxie'll be scared stiff. Let's get into the castle.'

Half an hour later, wrapped in towels and with a plate of jam scones on his knee, Nick asked the same question. His grandmother was on the telephone, telling the Sparrows and the Christians that their children would be staying the night at the castle.

'Why didn't Cain come after us? He'd never leave Qabahl alone to try for the Key.' Nick shrugged. 'I don't understand.'

'Neither do I, but I don't want to think about it,' Flip said. 'If I get miserable, I get wet.'

Flip sat in an armchair next to the fire, one hand gripping an umbrella and a circle of buckets catching the drips. Over his head, the cloud drizzled steadily. Wherever Flip went, the cloud went too. He had tried leaping through the lavatory door and slamming it, but the cloud just oozed under the door, more miserable than ever.

Bim ate her third scone. She and Maxie had borrowed Mrs Weston's dressing gowns and the warmth and the food had started to make them drowsy.

'It's the Show tomorrow.' Bim said. 'We won't have to miss it, will we? I think Dad was taking some cakes to sell.'

Nick became very still. 'I'd forgotten all about it. Weston's going to be full of people from all over the country. If the Door starts to move, it could do something terrible.' He swallowed two mouthfuls of tea, holding the hot mug to stop a sudden shiver. 'We'll have to go out and find it.'

Flip's cloud thundered and water bounced off the umbrella. Flip nodded. 'I know.'

We Three Kings

After breakfast, Flip found himself sitting in the library tower, his nose itching and his cloud hovering. He had hoped that the cloud would go during the night, but there it was, white and happy until it saw the look on his face. When it sulked, it darkened and fat drops of rain spattered Flip's head.

Nick touched his grandmother's shoulder. 'Grandma, I know what we are. I found the Weston diaries.'

'I see.' Mrs Weston shook her head. 'I would have told you, Nicholas, but your father stopped me. I should have known better.'

'My mother thought you were witches,' Flip said.

Mrs Weston laughed and some of the worry leaked from her face. 'No, we aren't witches. Have you heard of the Magi, Philip?'

Nick hummed. '"We three kings from orient are . . ."'

Flip's brows shot into his fringe. 'You mean the Three Wise Men?'

'One of our ancestors was a crusader,' Mrs Weston explained. 'He fought with King Richard, then studied the mysteries in Persia and married into one of the Magi families. The Westons have studied the world's secrets ever since.'

Flip gazed around the walls at the thousands of books, some so fragile that they lived in glass cases. They must be priceless.

'We're the librarians of the magic world,' Mrs Weston said. 'The people who come here add their own knowledge to our collection, so it's always growing. I think Nick explained about our Psychic Police?'

'They watch for my rockets,' Nick said. 'I fire green ones if everything's OK, red if we're in trouble.'

Less than a week ago, Flip had watched those green rockets from the shop. He had thought they were just pretty . . .

'We try not to use the PPs. They'd lock the books behind dangerous magic and no one would be able to read them. Our job is to help people read them, not to become jailors.' Mrs Weston frowned. 'I'm afraid the PPs don't see it that way.'

'But don't you have any powers yourself? You know, real powers?' Flip asked. 'When Typhoon comes here, can't you just do something?'

'Turn him into a frog?' Mrs Weston laughed. 'I'm afraid not. Any powers we have are in our minds, not for playing with sand.'

Bim rolled her eyes. 'I think it's really boring if you can't do real magic. Like making things fly.'

'You would,' Nick said. 'Anyway, however good Cain and Qabahl are, they aren't High Magicians.'

Mrs Weston explained. 'Merlin was the last High Magician in Britain. He could make something from nothing. Qabahl and Cain can't, and they need a ring or a wand to channel their powers. High Magicians use their own body.' She squeezed Nick's hand. 'What you don't know, Nicholas, is that the Magi saw a spark of old power in the Westons. That's why we're trusted to guard the oldest books.'

'You mean we might be able to do High Magic?' Nick frowned. 'High Magic's the real thing. Nothing like your Fixit Dust, Flip.'

Mrs Weston nodded. 'The Key's protected by High Magic so ordinary magic can't find it. Cain and Qabahl have to make whoever has it give it to them; they can't steal it with spells.'

'Qabahl will love that!' Nick said. Then he remembered something. 'Grandma, have you ever done anything to him? He said he was going to get even with you.'

'His family burnt our last home and two children died.' Her eyes misted and she blinked, made herself go on. 'When I die, there'll only be Nicholas to look after the castle. Qabahl laughed about the dying Weston family and I lost my temper and remembered a word of High Power. I used it to make him look stupid. He's a very dangerous enemy, Nicholas.'

The copper head of her stick nodded, 'He's a violent man.'

Bim yelped with shock.

Nick grinned at her. 'I once stood on it and it said "ouch".'

His grandmother lifted the stick so that the carved old man's head could look at them. Its copper eyes sparked with mischief and Mrs Weston smiled. 'He's my one and only magician's toy.'

Bim peered at it. It peered back at her. 'Now that's what I call magic! I wish I could take it to school. Can it do anything?'

The stick grinned at her. 'Not turn people into frogs, but I know a few things. For a start, I know why we're falling over brownies. Someone held the Key in the air and said "open". Instead of opening a real door, they opened the Door to the Other. That's the other side of everything real. And now the Door's blowing around, letting nasty things out. I'm afraid you'll have to find it and close it again.'

'But how do we find it?' Maxie rattled her beads. 'It could be anywhere.'

The stick gave a long, coppery sigh. 'The breeze came up during the night and it's blowing inland. The Door should be somewhere in the middle of the town. But if it was moving, everyone would see it. It must be somewhere out of sight or jammed so tight it can't move.'

'But what's it for?' Maxie frowned. 'And why was it just hanging around in the Sparrows' shop?'

'I don't know all the answers,' the stick said. 'The Key's as old as the Door, which is as old as the sky. No one knows why it came to the Sparrows, but they've always kept it safe. And there's no better way of hiding something valuable than hanging it on the back of a door on a dirty rope. Who'd look at it twice?'

'The magic is that there's only one Door, but the Key can open it anywhere.' Mrs Weston smiled. 'Even in the Sparrow kitchen. You see, only the High Magicians could travel through space and time by Magic. But if you jump through the Door to the Other, holding the Key, you can come out in any time or place you choose. You could go to the Jewel Room in the Tower of London or back in time to the Treasure Store of the Elven Kings. Believe me, the Key is priceless. Qabahl would kill to have it.'

'And you have to send everything that came out of the Door back to the Other side before you close it.' The stick chewed its bottom lip. 'Difficult. Very difficult.'

'If I was younger, I'd come with you.' Mrs Weston pushed the blond hair out of her grandson's eyes. 'But I'm a lame old woman and I can't chase the wind. Nicholas, take the stick and Sorath. A hawk's eyes are very sharp. He might find the Door before the others do.'

'The show!' Flip suddenly knew. 'The Door will be at the show. We did it in geography. It's the shape of the cliffs around Weston. A freak wind blows in towards the coast then goes around the park. That's why the bay's so good for wind-surfing.'

The stick stared at him. 'He's right. The Door will be somewhere in St Brigid's Park. There are hundreds of trees in that place. It could be stuck anywhere.'

'And if we can think of that, so can Cain and Qabahl.' Nick stood up. 'We'd better get going.'

His grandmother nodded. 'I'll get Hopkins to drive you.'

'Qabahl could try to grab us again.' Bim pulled a face. 'I don't suppose he'll turn into a crocodile in the middle of the show, unless he pretends he's in the fancy dress . . .'

'I'd forgotten about the fancy dress.' Mrs Weston's dark eyes widened. 'Most of the children in Weston will enter the competition. If you're in fancy dress as well, you might fool Cain and Qabahl, even if it only wins you a few seconds. Let's see what we've got to fit you all.'

The Westons' collection of old play clothes and fancy dress would have filled a shop. Maxie became an Eastern princess, all glittering, golden trousers and top, a veil hiding her nose and chin. Nick wore tartan and an orange wig and strode around saying, 'Och, aye, Jimmy.' Giggling, Bim stuffed her curls

108

under a spotted scarf, pulled an eye-patch over one eye and dressed as a pirate.

'This is ace!' She jumped up and down in the big boots. 'I should always dress like this.'

Nick twanged her eye-patch. 'No, I can still see some of your face.'

Flip became a pink-fur rabbit with a fluffy cloud over his head.

'Right, we're ready, then.' Flip looked down his long pink legs to the furry white feet. 'I feel a right wally . . . Still, I can run in it, if I have to. And it's got pockets for all my magic stuff.'

'Oh no!' Nick groaned. 'Flip, don't start that again!'

'Nick, we'll need all the help we can get. But I'd better test the Invisible Dust first, just to see if it works.'

Nick yelled and tried to duck but Flip was too quick. A cloud of grey shimmer wafted over him. 'Oh great! Really great! Why do you always pick on me?'

Bim scowled. 'It didn't work. I can still see him.'

'Well, I can't see you.' Nick waved his arms around, trying to get rid of the dust. 'All I can see is grey.'

'Something must have gone wrong,' Flip said. 'But it's only dust.' He dug his pink furry toes into the carpet. The cloud snuffled a few drips onto his shoulders. 'Maybe you can walk out of it.'

Eyes staring at nothing, Nick walked forwards. And blinked. And gave Flip a cold stare. 'Very clever. Can we go now?'

'Spoilsport,' Flip said. 'But I'm still taking the weather machine in the car. You never know, we might need it.'

The strange party hurried out of the castle to where

109

Hopkins waited with the Westons' open-topped car. Flip and Nick bundled the weather machine on to the back seat, then crammed after it, Sorath curling his talons into Nick's tartan shoulder and squealing. Above his pink rabbit ears, Flip's cloud fluffed with excitement.

The Door had arrived at the show. Three police cars flew through the main entrance and Mr Hopkins slammed his brakes on just in time. 'Ruddy idiot drivers! I wonder what's going on in there?'

Nick watched the people run out of the food tent. 'I can guess.'

He launched Sorath and the hawk climbed until it was a black smudge against the sky. A fresh breeze blew sweet papers over the grass. If the Door was not moving, it must be well and truly stuck.

Mrs Weston had been right about wearing fancy dress. The park overflowed with superheroes, gypsies and spacemen. A few people gulped at the pink rabbit with the pet cloud but no one stopped to stare.

'Let's stick together.' Flip pulled Bim away from the hot-dog van. 'We'll walk around and hope the Door starts moving. Keep a look out for Typhoon and Cain.'

The Door had definitely arrived at the show. The gardening tent had the first blue-leafed rose with orange flowers in the world and the first purple tomatoes. Next door, the police chased two dozen brownies around the food tent as the hairy bodies gobbled prize scones and what was left of Mr Sparrow's best wedding cake.

'All right, then. Let's check towards the lake.' Flip hunched his furry shoulders until they tickled his ears. 'That's where the wind blows.'

Maxie trotted beside him, gold trousers glittering.

110

'Don't you think we'd have heard something if the Door suddenly appeared? People'd go crazy.'

'I know.' Flip shook his head. 'No one said this was going to be easy. Where's that bird, Nick? Nick . . .? Oh no! He's gone off . . .' Flip groaned and his cloud darkened. 'Let's split up and start looking for him. He can't have gone far.' Then under his breath, 'I hope.'

The small tent hid in the shadow of the park café, its door-flap fluttering welcome. The poster outside said 'Holograms. See our unique light show.' A flat piece of plastic just under the sign became a beckoning finger as the light caught it. Another held a winking eye. Another was a circle in a circle, slowly turning and changing from blue to green to blue. Spinning . . .

The stick groaned. 'Nicholas, you must concentrate! You've lost the others. Nicholas . . .?'

The blue and green slid inside Nick's head, spinning and spinning. He hardly saw the hand that dragged him into the darkness. Hardly felt the metal circles tighten around his arms. Around his legs. The hand held a spinning light in front of his eyes and he could not move any more.

'Sit down.' Cold, cold voice. 'And now, Nicholas Weston, you'll tell me everything I want to know.'

Only that cold voice penetrated the metal ring of power surrounding the low stool. The other circles held Nick's body, but the voice held his mind. Ice-cold fingers gripped his brain and he could not think at all.

The stick bumped up and down in Nick's hand. 'Don't look at him! Don't listen . . . Nicholas!!'

111

Cain snatched the stick out of Nick's limp hand and threw it on to the grass. Then he lifted one foot and deliberately ground the copper face into the soil, forced choking lumps of clay into the copper mouth.

'Four kids, a lump of wood and a wild bird.' Cain stepped back into the circle of power. 'It's pathetic. Your grandmother's too old to catch me, Nicholas, and you don't know enough to even slow me down. So tell me where the Key is. Your skinny friend had it yesterday, but it's never been in range today. I'm sick of playing games, so you'd better tell me, right now.'

'No . . .' Eyes blank, arms aching against the tight metal, Nick still knew that he could not tell. He did not know why any more, but it was important that he did not tell this sharp-smiling man about the Key. He managed to shake his head. 'No . . .'

'In that case, one of my little circles is going to tighten around your head until it cracks like an egg. Look at me . . . look me in the eye.'

Horrible eyes. Nick shivered, struggling to move away, but he could not. His arms hurt badly. The dead-fish eyes tried to see into his head.

'No—'

The stick spat soil, helplessly, hating the taste and the smell. The smell? No one's feet smelled that strong. Flip! It tried to yell but its throat had swollen shut. There was only one thing to do. It jammed its eyes shut, gritted its teeth and shrieked through its nose. Cups shattered in the café next door. Plates split in half and teapots exploded as Flip leapt through the tent door.

'I knew it!' Flip gasped for breath. 'I knew it would be you. Let Nick go! Or I'll yell so loud everyone'll come running, all the photographers, everyone.

112

You'll be all over the front page tomorrow—'

Suddenly Flip's cloud boiled black, thundered and began to rain on Flip's rabbit ears. Cain's fish eyes bulged. 'Nick, I think he's going to zap me! Nick, wake up!'

No brilliant ideas came into Flip's head this time. The cloud spat lightning and hit Flip's pocket.

'Ow! Not me, you stupid—'

His pocket! With a yell, Flip grabbed everything in his pocket, ripped the paper and threw the lot at Cain's shark teeth.

A heavy mass of dust and crystals filled the tent. The stench of Smelly Foot Powder drove Flip for the floor. Hand on nose, he crawled to where Nick ought to be. The Invisible Dust was everywhere and he could not see a thing. And he croaked. His hands croaked, his knees croaked. The world was a grey mass of dizzy, toad-croaking stink. All he could think of was breaking the rings around Nick with soil, like Nick had done when the two magicians were fighting. He knelt on the stick.

'Flip!' the stick yelped, and sneezed. 'Use me to feel around. Find the metal ring.'

Flat on his stomach, Flip swung the stick over the grass. Cain blundered past, cursing terribly but as blind as Flip. And for the first time all day, the cloud did not try to follow its master.

Another swish of the stick and its copper head met the metal ring of power. The stick bit through it and the spell broke.

'Nick!' Flip heard him groaning awake. 'Nick, I'm coming!'

Eyes shut, Flip took a chance, launched himself and crashed into Nick's back. Somehow he got a shoulder under Nick's arm, then he peered around,

113

lost in the grey world of Invisible Dust. At the door to the tent, thundering and flashing, his pet cloud was a beacon. Flip grinned and dragged Nick backwards, aiming for the angry lightning.

'Nick, we're nearly out,' Flip gasped, feet croaking. 'You weigh a ton!'

'Sorry. I'm dizzy.' Nick sneezed. 'What's that horrible smell?'

'Us. Come on!'

They staggered outside into a circle of startled people. People holding their noses in horror. Nick's orange wig fell off and he sagged on to his knees. They croaked.

'Nick?'

'I'm OK, Flip.' Nick shivered and hugged his ribs, gathering his strength. 'One thing about being a Magus, though. No one ever fools you the same way twice. Your cloud's back.'

Fluffy white with relief, the cloud bobbed above Flip's pink ears.

'Oh no!' Nick stared down at his hands. 'Flip! You twit! Look at us!'

He looked up and Flip saw the red dots all over his face and remembered the False Measles. 'There wasn't time to be choosy, Nick. I threw everything.'

'Great. Just great,' Nick said. 'I suppose we're lucky you didn't throw Three-legs Powder. We stink like athlete's socks!'

Then he stopped grumbling and listened. Screams came from the direction of the fair.

'That's it! Flip, that's the Door!' Nick yelled and sprinted off, kilt flapping. Flip pushed the stick into his rabbit suit and ran after him.

Nightmare Funfair

'Flip!' Bim skidded into his feet. 'Flip, the wind's changed! Woooww! I saw one!'

A dark streak curled from behind the food tent.

'That one was the darkest yet, so it's getting stronger.' Flip shook his head. 'It's getting worse.'

'Pooohhh!' Bim suddenly recoiled, hand on nose. 'Flip! You stink! And you're covered in spots!'

Flip glared at her. 'My feet croak as well, so shut up!'

They ran out of the park and through the iron gates into the funfair. The fairground had become a nightmare. Screaming people ducked as dark jets swept through the stalls like a lightless fire-work display.

The big merry-go-round had gone mad. A dark comet had changed its bright horses into red-eyed, teeth-snapping beasts and children clung to their plunging backs, crying with fright as the ride spun faster.

'Someone's going to get hurt,' Nick said. 'One of those kids is going to let go. They can't hold on at that speed.'

Flip gripped his arm. 'The weather machine.'

Nick nodded. 'I'll climb on top and pedal. You point the wings.'

Nick struggled into the car and up the larger bicycle wheel. Hanging at an angle, the machine creaked ominously and he had to hold the handle-bars with both hands to keep upright. A frantic leap on to the box of magnets and he pedalled furiously. Flip moved the tin-can wings to catch the sun. Humming, sparking energy rattled the magnets and the old umbrella spokes glowed pink.

'Now!' Flip pointed the umbrella at the spinning horses and white light flashed over the car. 'Jump, Nick!'

They jumped clear as the umbrella snapped shut. A beam of pink light cracked from its spokes and sprayed the roundabout with glittering sequins of light. Pink ice crystals crept into the motor, into the small spaces between the spinning wheels, into the very heart of the machinery. Pink snow fell on the wild horses, melting and steaming. More fell and the steam faded, the snow taking hold. Slowly, savage manes hardened, foam-spattered teeth sagged shut and hot horseflesh turned back into painted wood. The ride juddered to a halt and everyone rushed forwards, climbing on to the ride to help the crying children slide free.

'Cain and Qabahl will be here any minute. They're bound to know what's happening.' Nick knocked a layer of pink snow from his shoulders. Smelly Foot powder stank twice as bad when it was wet . . . 'This stink's making me sick. They could find us by following the pong!'

'Or the croaks,' Bim said. 'Every time you move, something croaks.'

Then Nick felt it coming. 'Hang on! Hang on to something!'

The wind flared incredibly strong, throwing people face-down in the snow. Horizontal, clinging to the

116

steering wheel for dear life, Flip felt the Door sail over his head. His fur ears flapped wildly, and his cloud was sucked away. All around him, fairground people and holiday-makers slid in the pink slush and fell. The snow built up in drifts around the foot of the roundabout and froze on eyelashes and beards. And the wind died. It had gone. And the Door to the Other had gone with it.

Bim dragged the stick out of the snow. 'Where does the wind go when it stops blowing?'

Beside the car, a pink drift shuddered and blond hair and measles spots appeared. Nick stood up and shook himself like a dog, then whistled. Sorath swooped down to his shoulder, feathers wind-ruffled but still strong, eager to fly. When Nick stroked his wings, he tossed his head and squealed.

The stick frowned for a moment and nodded. 'To the place where all the old ships used to blow.'

Nick's brows rose. 'The island? Are you sure?'

'That wind was old. When old winds die, they try to take something with them. So they steal ships or anything else needing wind to move.' The stick shook its head. 'We're lucky it only took the Door . . .'

'It took my cloud!' Flip felt robbed. He missed the stupid thing already. 'And how can a wind be old? You're not telling me you can get the same wind twice?'

'More than twice,' the stick said. 'They live for many years, getting stronger as they get older, until they die in a last gust of air. Quite sad, really.'

Two metres away, hiding behind a crisp packet, a small fly did not think a dead wind was sad. It did not think at all, just looked and listened and it had heard enough. Sandy wings buzzing, it flew over the fairground to where a black car waited.

117

'That was a sand fly.'

Everyone turned to stare at Nick.

'How're we supposed to do anything without them knowing if they can put sand flies near us!' Nick kicked at the snow angrily. 'And any patch of light or circle of metal could be Cain's magic . . . It's impossible!'

Suddenly he gasped. 'Flip! Freckles!'

'Eh?'

'Don't move!' Nick's thumb stabbed Flip on the nose.

Flip flinched. 'Hey, what was that for!'

'Look. He planted this on you.' A minute, golden ring lay on Nick's palm, like a small freckle. 'He's been looking through this all the time. Wherever we went, he was watching the rest of us from your nose!' Nick twisted and threw the ring into the sea.

'Don't give up so easily, Nicholas.' The stick smiled at his stiff, measle-spotted face. 'We can always use their magic against them.' Nick wandered on to the beach and the others followed.

Bim's scowl knotted black brows above her nose. It meant that Bim was thinking very hard. Sometimes, that hurt. 'We could use these as well.' She dug into her pirate-coat and pulled out a bunch of keys.

Nick blinked. 'Where did you get those . . .? I've seen some of them before.'

'I asked your grandma. You see, if Typhoon or Cain get one of these and think it's the real Key, they'll stop chasing us.' She shrugged, enjoying everyone's open-mouthed shock. 'Well, I thought it was a good idea.'

'Bim,' Nick smiled at her sweetly. 'How're we going to fool them into thinking one of those is the real Key?'

Bim shrugged. 'I can't think of everything. But it's worth a try. And anyway, we haven't got time to think of anything else. We have to get to the island before something terrible comes out of the Door.'

'I know. It's just so . . .'

The train grazed past Nick's back. Flip sprawled over a deserted sandcastle.

The Tiny Tots Wagontrain had left its circle of track ten minutes before. It had rattled its row of white-covered wagons halfway along the Prom and back and now it enjoyed the sand. Each wagon had two seats under the flapping roof and a pair of reins to pretend horses.

Maxie's eyes widened. 'I know! We can open the water, like Moses and the Red Sea!'

Flip stared at her. 'Hey! Hey, that might work.' He tossed her the Key. 'It's your turn, Max. See if it will go right to the island.'

'Come on then!' She bounded over the cold froth, knee-deep into the water. 'Open. To the island.'

Salt water rippled around Maxie's legs. It swirled and bubbled and started to open out before her. Instead of foam, Maxie stood on wet sand. The bubbling changed to leaping spouts of sea-water and a narrow path pushed out from the beach, sizzling with power between the cold waves.

'It's working.' Bim jumped up and down. 'Look at it!'

A finger of sand slid through the sea. Water walls rose on either side and a long corridor grew into the distance, stretching nearly three miles to the island.

The wagon train headed back towards them and Nick snapped his fingers. 'That's it! It would take too long to walk. Let's take the wagons. Sorath, fly! Find

119

the Door.' Nick ran towards the lead wagon, grabbed the side and vaulted in. 'Come on!'

'Oh well,' Flip shrugged. 'Wait, Nick!' He threw himself into the back of the wagon, sat up and put his head through the cotton roof. 'Oh, brilliant!'

Bim scrambled into the second wagon, giggling. Maxie hopped neatly beside her, then leaned over the back and disconnected the other wagons.

'Here we go.' Nick pulled the reins towards the sea. 'The first half's downhill. It might be bumpy.'

The Sea and the Island

The wagons bounced on to the wet sand, sea-water on both sides. Waves lapped at knee level, then at neck level, then higher than the white-cotton roofs. Thick, grey-glass walls of water made a sort of canyon in the sea. No one spoke. No one would have heard a word, anyway. Salt water groaned and splashed and the wagon wheels crushed broken bottles, coke tins, all the rubbish that people had thrown into the sea.

'Fish . . .' Flip pointed at the ghostly bodies behind the walls. No one heard him. 'FISH!!' he yelled.

'I know they're fish!' Nick yelled back. 'Dumbo!'

The sea bed sloped steeply and the wagons jolted faster. Each bounce took Flip's head through the roof. His arms ached with hanging on to the wagon seat but he hardly noticed. He was under the sea, hypnotised by the silver flashes of fish in the dark water. All he could think of was his dad's camera and how he wished it had been here. Larger fish banged and barged and tried to get through the walls. Their glassy eyes peered at him. It was like being inside a television set, looking out at the audience. He glimpsed twisted planks that must have been shipwrecks. A rusty anchor touched the wall

121

and its chain crunched under the wagon's wheels.

Nick squeezed Flip's arm and mouthed, 'Look, the first wrecks.'

And no camera! Flip nearly cried as they rattled past the sunken steam-ship. The metal plates had rusted and some of the bolts had worn away. The ship lay on its side, funnels half buried in the mud and sand. Seaweed tangled the ship's rail where passengers must have stood, gazing over the ocean. As the wagons clattered away, Flip saw the massive tear in the boat's side. The metal curled back from the long hole like an opened sardine tin. Even years under the waves had not washed away the black stain of fire. People had died in there.

As the seabed started to rise, wrecks crowded the rocky ground. Some were so old that the wood had worn to powder. Others were from World War II, grey-metal jutting out of the dark-green sea. And a single aeroplane that Flip recognized as a Spitfire lay in one piece, a shoal of fish playing around its broken cockpit.

Watery light reached down into the split in the sea. When Flip looked up, he glimpsed a pale slash of sky. He clung on as the wagons climbed upwards.

Bim sneezed just as her wagon hit a rock. She thudded on to Maxie's legs and her elbow jabbed the Key into Maxie's stomach.

'Ow! Bim, be careful. Sit still.'

'I'm trying!' Bim's voice cracked, trying to yell over the crash of waves. 'I wish those waves would shut up—!'

Her elbow had been touching the Key. As soon as she said 'shut', the water-walls quivered. Spray splashed over the cotton roofs, over Flip's rabbit ears and Nick's tartan shoulder.

'Bim! Oh no . . .'

The walls shuddered and heaved. Salt water rained down.

'Can you swim, Nick?' Flip saw Nick nod. 'Max, can you swim?'

Maxie nodded as well and saw Bim's eyes turn glassy with horror. 'Don't worry, Bim, I'll help you.'

The sea flooded the sides of the wall and swirled up under the wagons. Wild water threw them skywards and everyone hung on, praying that the walls would hold for just a few minutes longer. Sheets of cold foam tore the cotton roofs from their metal frames.

'Hang on!!' Flip took a deep breath, then water smashed him into the bottom of the wagon. A massive weight held him, struggling, too afraid to breathe, waves above him, underneath him, all around him. Drowning him. He kicked and kicked and found the edge of the wood and kicked again. And shot to the surface, the air-filled rabbit-suit better than any life-jacket. 'Yurgh . . . Groooo . . .' He spat water, dog-paddling for dear life. He could not see anything for his wet fringe. 'Nick?! Maxie . . .?!'

Nick spluttered up beside him. 'Bim is a twit,' he said and coughed up a mouthful of water.

Maxie's beads appeared, then her plaits, then her dark face, gasping for breath. A mighty heave and she yanked Bim on to the surface by the hair. Bim had not been as clean in months.

Nick glared at her. 'You're a twit, Sparrow!'

The stick floated beside him, carefully keeping its head above the waves. 'Save your breath for swimming, Nicholas. Philip, you're going to fill with water if that fur soaks through.'

123

'I'll be OK. If it gets heavy, I'll unzip it.'

The island waited, black and spiny in a white haze of spray.

Jagged and treacherous, the shore of the island rose from the water in pillars of rock. No one expected a soft landing. They launched themselves through the surf and scraped upwards, gasping and clawing for hand-holds. Nick threw his arms around a narrow ridge and locked them tight as the sea surged back again. Flip clung to Nick's ankles and Bim drove her fingers under Flip's belt. Maxie wedged herself in a gulley and shut her eyes until the water had swept over her.

'Come on before the next wave,' Flip grunted as Bim trod on his knee. 'Max, you OK?'

Maxie nodded and crawled past, her gold trousers in shreds.

'Sorath must be here already.' Nick jumped over the rock on to a mound of shingle. 'I'll run ahead and see if I can find him.'

'No!' Slithering out of control, Flip oofed on to the pebbles. 'Nick, don't you dare . . . Rest or you'll drop. You know what you're like. You never feel tired till it flattens you.'

Nick pulled a face. 'You sound like my Grandma.' But he nodded and followed the others off the beach. 'At least the swim's washed all that dust off. I'm not croaking any more. And the measle spots have gone.'

Bim sniffed. 'You still pong a bit.'

They flopped on to the first patch of rough grass. Without the sunlight, the air was bitter cold and their wet clothes stuck to their skin.

Bim's teeth rattled and she shuddered. 'How're we going to get back? Has anyone thought?' No one answered and she fell into a silent sulk. Then she sat up. 'There isn't any sand! It's all rock and pebbles! Typhoon can't use his sand magic.'

The stick sighed. 'No, Beverley. But he'll find something else to use.

Flip grunted and pulled a hard lump from under his hip. It looked like white plastic. 'I don't like this place.' He tossed the lump from hand to hand. 'It's real spooky.'

'It's haunted.' Nick rolled on to his back. 'All the wrecks come here. People say you can hear the dead ships crying in the night. That's probably a bone you're playing with.'

Flip gulped and dropped it. 'You mean human bone . . .?' He winced. 'No, forget I said anything. Come on, we'll freeze if we keep still. I don't like the look of those clouds.'

Not a breath of breeze moved over the wreck-covered boulders. As the children clambered away from the sea, the silence spread around them.

The hawk found them almost at the heart of the island, in a dark crevice between rocky walls. It flew down to Nick's wrist.

'He's been all over the island and there's no sign of the Door. It must be stuck somewhere. I wish . . .' He stopped, frowning. 'I wish I could remember.'

'Remember what?' Flip asked.

'I can't remember.'

Flip rolled his eyes. 'Nick, don't start . . .'

'I'm not playing around, Flip. Honestly.' Nick shook his head. 'It's hard to explain. Westons pass their memories from father to son to daughter . . . Like you might get blue eyes because blue eyes run in the family, we get memories because our memories run in the family. I know a Weston's been here and

I'm trying to remember what he saw . . .' He shut his eyes, wiping his mind. 'It's north. There's something on the north side of the island . . . a cliff—' he shrugged. 'I'm sorry, that's all.'

'OK.' Flip looked at Bim and Maxie, saw them nod. 'Let's go north.'

As Maxie led the way on to the cliff top the first drop of rain splotted her nose. Suddenly, the stick jumped in Bim's fist. 'Something's leaking out of the ground . . . Stop! The ground's not safe! Maxie, stop!'

Bim yelled. 'Stop, Maxie!'

Maxie screamed. A dark rush of air tore out of the ground at her feet, slammed into a dead tree and exploded in black flames. Lumps of burnt wood scattered over the cliff and the stony soil slid and crumbled. Maxie screamed again as the cliff broke apart. And Nick dived, knocking her in the middle of the back. Flip caught her as the ground fell away. He saw Nick throw both arms out, snatching for any hand-hold. It was no use. Nick vanished in a crashing river of rock.

Silence. Dust rose from the hole in choking clouds.

'Can you see him?' The stick craned its copper neck to look over the edge. 'Nicholas?'

Bim sneezed and peered into the dust. 'You all right, Nick?'

'No!' Nick's voice floated up to them. 'Owww . . .!'

The dust slowly cleared. A jumble of broken rocks appeared, chunks of soil and burnt tree . . . Wincing, Nick slithered on to flat ground and nursed his ankle.

Bim nodded. 'He's all right.'

'Stop saying I'm all right!' Nick glared up at her, face grey with dust. 'I've got bruises on my bruises. But I know what I was trying to remember.'

Sorath dropped into the hole like a stone, screeching on to Nick's shoulder. He rubbed his curved beak against Nick's chin.

'I'm OK, Sorath.' Nick soothed the bird's tawny feathers. 'Flip, it's a cave. The whole rock's hollow. There are tunnels everywhere and I can feel a breeze. That's what I wanted to remember. The island's full of caves.'

'Right. Let's all go down.' Flip crawled to the smoothest part of the slope. 'I bet the Door's in one of those caves. I'll go first. Try not to slide too fast or you'll cut yourself.'

He slid feet first over the rocks and the others followed. They tried to be careful but the dribbles of stony soil moved under their feet and they skidded and stumbled. By the time they had reached the bottom of the slide, they were grazed red.

Nick had scraped the dust from his face and his chin had a nice bruise on it, but he was grinning. 'Don't worry, I can walk. But I'd better use the stick, just in case. I'm a bit wobbly.'

The cave opened in front of them, bigger than the school hall, an arched roof of black and grey rock over a gritty floor. The grit had blown in from the beach, which meant that some of the tunnels leading from the cave had to open on to the sea. As Flip strode forwards, he heard distant waves shatter on rock.

Bim bounced into the air. 'This is great!'

'. . . is great . . . is great . . . is great . . .' The echo sang back at her.

'Hi! I'm Bim!'

'. . . Bim . . . Bim . . . Bim . . .'

'Bim, shut up!'

'. . . up . . . up . . . up.'

127

If the roof had not fallen in, the huge space would have been dark. Cold light shone through the new hole and threw crooked shadows from their feet. Bim grinned at her shadow and made it curl its shoulders like a gorilla. Sorath swept from tunnel to tunnel, his sharp eyes searching for the smallest trace of blue light. At the very last opening, he found it. He squealed and flew into the stone passage.

'In there!' Nick slapped the top of Bim's head. 'Come on, follow him.'

Behind Nick's foot, the rock moved, opened a single eye and blinked. Then it closed and turned into footprints running up the wall to fetch its master.

Through the Door

They hurried into the tunnel, Nick leaning on the stick to take some of the weight from his ankle, Flip and Maxie keeping an ear open for anyone following them. The tunnel curved away from the big cave in a steep spiral through the rock. The sound of the sea filled it, echoing hungrily.

'How long do you think it is, Nick?'

'A couple of kilometres, maybe. Hard to tell, it's too curly.' He slithered and had to throw both hands out to save himself. 'I'd hate to have to run in it. These bits of grit are like marbles.'

'Want to slow down?'

'No, I'll be fine. I can see blue ahead.'

Flickering blue lit the wall in flashes, dying down, then flaring again. From the Door. About ten minutes later, the tunnel curled sideways and out through an arch of rock.

'Wow!' Flip's feet rooted to the ground. 'Wow!' he said, then nothing else. He could not believe what he was seeing.

'It's probably a smuggler's ship,' Nick decided. 'There were a lot of smugglers on this coast.'

The tunnel ended in a cave so large it made the other one look like a small hole. Its roof stretched as high as the cliff-top and plunged down into the water. A narrow gap in the rock-wall led to the open sea and white foam crashed in from the breaking waves.

The ship must have been caught in a violent storm. It had been carried towards the island and some freak wave had lifted it straight through the jagged doorway. Both of its masts had split and the tangled topsails hung over the deck in a mass of rigging. The ship's hull rocked very gently in the dark water. As it moved, the door flared sky-blue and spat black comets and ribbons of fire. Darkness crept over the ship like grey fingers.

'Listen.' Bim scowled. 'What's that?'

'It's a speed boat.'

The stick groaned. 'I'm a fool! Cain will have maps of this whole area. He was bound to look for the caves sooner or later. We must get to the ship first.'

Suddenly another noise swept towards the cave, this time from behind. Massively clawed feet scrabbled down the tunnel, dragging a heavy body and swinging tail over the rock. Sparks and cracks of raw evil slashed the darkness of the tunnel mouth. It was Qabahl.

'He wants me as much as the Key. If I'm in his way, he won't be able to resist attacking me.' Nick tried to get past Flip's arms. 'Let me past, Flip. I'll give you time to get to the Door.'

'No way!' Flip shook his head angrily. 'Don't start that again! It's stupid! No one's going to get hurt. I won't let them.'

Maxie squeezed Nick's shoulder. 'You can't, Nick. He might kill you. Flip, let's get all the keys out. We'll close our eyes and take one each. Then only the person who's got the real Key will know.

130

Bim undid the bunch of keys. Five keys plopped into five different pockets.

'Now, let's try to get to the ship.'

Loose stones rattled down the tunnel. As Flip stepped on to the ledge over the water, a great smouldering rush of air lifted him off his feet. He sprawled on the rock, both hands over his head, feeling his wrists burn. Behind him, the giant crocodile stretched its jaws in a deafening scream. And Nick jumped over Flip's legs, putting himself between Qabahl and the others.

Qabahl watched Nick through slit-eyes. Half-man, half-crocodile, standing as tall as a man but scale-fleshed, his eyes burnt from hard wedges of skin. Without a word, he spun his stick across the cave wall. Rock turned to sand. Before Nick could shout a warning, the cave walls slid in a dusty river, flowing over Flip and Maxie, covering Bim, churning with arms and legs.

'No! Stop it!' Nick threw himself at the scaly creature. 'Don't . . . They're suffocating!'

'And I'll let them suffocate . . .' Qabahl's jaws widened, breathing rotten-flesh breath over Nick's face. 'I want the real Key and now, or I'll bury them a mile deep!'

'I've got it . . . Take it . . . Just stop . . . Let them go.' Nick could not think. Terrified, he leapt on to the pile of sand, scraping armfuls away, desperately. 'Please! I'll give you anything you want, just help them . . .!'

The sand stopped.

Crying, Nick attacked the hill of sand, scraping and scraping, coughing at the dust in his throat, pulling arms and legs until Flip spluttered free. Then Maxie . . .

'Bim! I can't find Bim!' Nick drove his hands down but he could not find her . . . 'Flip, help. She can't breathe down there . . .'

Bim's left elbow cracked Nick on the chin, then red curls cascaded a waterfall of sand, shooting upwards as if they were on springs. Bim spat, then took a deep breath. She opened her eyes. 'I held my breath,' she said.

A clawed hand gripped Nick's shoulder and lifted him until his feet kicked in mid-air. 'If you're messing me around this time, I'll tear your head off. Where's the Key?'

Bim stepped forwards, bottom lip stuck out. 'I've got it. You can have it . . . Just let Nick go.'

'Bim . . .!' Nick shuddered, feeling Qabahl's red eyes narrow.

'So you've got it, have you, Weston? Liar!' He swung Nick over the edge of the drop. 'I should have known you'd lie through your teeth.'

Bim looked at Nick and gave a funny little shrug. 'Here it is, then.'

Qabahl snatched the small silver key and dragged Nick back on to the ledge. 'Now walk. We're going to the ship.'

'He's going to take me through the Door!' Nick yelled. He looked terrified, starting to kick and squirm in Qabahl's hand. 'He'll never let me go . . .'

Qabahl laughed and lifted the struggling boy higher. Then his hard fingers closed around Nick's neck.

'You'd still try to trick me, wouldn't you? So I'm not going to give you the chance.' His eyes flared brilliant red and his crocodile teeth glittered. 'Sutekh Eset Khepera Bes!'

Nick shivered and crumpled like a piece of torn

132

cloth. Shrieking with laughter, Qabahl straightened his arm and threw Nick head first off the ledge. The boy's body plummetted, crashing on to a heap of fallen sails. Dust ballooned over the ship's deck and Qabahl jumped into it, screeching his triumph.

The speed-boat roared into the cave, Cain's plump face behind the wheel.

'You're too late, Cain!' Qabahl ran to the ship's rail to gloat. 'I have the Key!'

Behind Qabahl's legs, dark steam pushed through the ship's timbers, spreading over the deck like smoke. The ship groaned and tilted.

'Avast there! Wheel to port!' Nick yelled. He rolled over the deck as the ship tilted.

Qabahl slid backwards, his crocodile-man body top heavy, dragging him towards the Door. Cursing, screaming, he dug his claws into the wood, trying to find anything to hold on to. His fingers clutched at nothing and he skidded through the Door. For a second, his snarling teeth hung in the air, then he vanished.

'Come on!' Flip ran along the ledge. 'Quick!' He launched himself, rabbit-ears flapping, into the pile of sails. Maxie followed, then Bim. It was a long way down and the deck groaned with the impact.

Nick tried to turn but could not pull his feet away from the old woodwork. One of Cain's rings was round his ankles and his feet were glued to the deck.

Cain struggled on to the ship, panting and shaking his head. 'Clever! Very clever! I underestimated you, Nicholas . . . getting rid of poor Qabahl. You understood all of his Egyptian charms, didn't you?'

Nick's fingers flew through his shoelaces, pulled them loose . . . No use. His feet were stuck in his shoes and his shoes were stuck to the deck. He stood up again, wincing at the dreadful cold in Cain's smile. 'I understood them. I just couldn't read them.'

'Of course, you're dyslexic. I'd forgotten.' Cain lifted his arm. 'I wonder if you can read this?'

It was a reflex to look at Cain's hand. Flip tried to run forwards but scattered light blinded him, gold rings caught his ankles and held him. Maxie and Bim found themselves locked to the ship's rail.

Cain smiled as blue and green light flickered over Nick's face. 'You gave Qabahl the wrong key, didn't you?'

Nick nodded, eyes too wide, glued to the spinning light.

'So, who's got the real one?'

'I have,' Nick said, and pulled the long iron key from his kilt pocket, letting it dangle on its dirty loop of rope.

Cain took the Key, smiled and gave Nick a vicious kick that bowled him over the deck.

'When I get what I want from the Other World, no one will dare get in my way. Not the Psychic Police, not your dear grandmother, no one. I'll enjoy burning your castle to the ground, Nicholas. And I'll keep your books for myself. If I was you . . .' And his shark-smile widened. 'If I was you, Nicholas Weston, I'd run as fast as I could and keep on running. For the rest of my life!'

Cain turned on his heel and stepped through the Door. His cold smile floated there, faded and vanished. Golden rings disappeared and Cain's magic left This Side.

Bim's brows knotted over her nose. 'Nick . . .?'

Terrible sadness twisted Nick's face. For about three seconds. He could not help himself, he burst into fits of laughter. 'That was the key to the outside bog!'

The stick closed its eyes. 'Nicholas! If I had a heart, it would have stopped!'

Flip collapsed on to the ship's rail. 'I thought you were hypnotised!'

'Of course you did,' Nick shrugged. 'It wouldn't have been much good if you could tell I was pretending. I told you, you can't fool a Magus twice with the same trick. Cain forgot.'

Half way to Nick's side, Flip caught a glimpse of something grey and damp lurking behind the deck house. 'Oh no!'

The cloud recognized the giant pink rabbit and whizzed across the deck, fluffing and bubbling with happiness.

'Oh no!' Flip gazed up at the cotton-wool white. 'I thought it had gone for good! Look at it!'

Nick grinned at him. 'It's hard not to. You taking it home with you?'

The cloud waited, grey at the edges, while Flip frowned. A tiny drop of rain plopped between his pink ears and Flip sighed. 'Oh, I suppose so . . . I suppose I could housetrain it or something . . .'

'I'll buy you an umbrella for Christmas,' Nick said. 'Now, you've got the real Key, haven't you, Maxie? Shut the Door.'

'And leave them all on the Other Side?' Flip shook his head. 'We can't do that!'

'Why not?'

'Nick!' Flip groaned. 'Come on, you know we can't.'

Bim scowled. 'I think Nick's right.'

'Well, you would.'

135

'So do I,' Maxie shivered. 'They're bad men. If they got out, they'd just go on being bad.'

Flip gazed at the three faces. Even the stick frowned, not sure what to say. He tried again. 'Look, it might serve Typhoon and Cain right to be stuck on the Other Side, but would it serve the Other Side right? There might be a few nice people in there. The dwarfs aren't all bad, are they? How'd you feel if someone dropped Typhoon into your back yard?'

Nick frowned. 'You've got a point there.'

'Whatever we do, we've still got to get all the things that came out of the Door back inside,' Maxie said. 'And everyone will be worrying about us. Please let's go home.'

'We've got the Key and the Door together,' Flip thought out loud. 'That means we can go anywhere, doesn't it?'

The stick nodded. 'Anywhere, anytime, Philip.'

'Well, everyone will be in the Park listening to Mrs Weston's speech at the show. We should go there.'

Nick glanced at the Key in Maxie's hand. 'There's no hurry, is there? We can get there whenever we want.'

Flip stepped back, warily. 'What are you up to?'

'Up to?' Nick widened his eyes. 'Me?'

'Oh come on!'

Nick grinned. 'All right . . . Just all stand together and keep very still. We're going to move really fast and through time as well. I don't want to ruin Grandma's speech.'

'You mean we'll get there before we got here?' Flip's brain refused to think about it. 'That's really weird.'

Nick shrugged. 'I suppose it is, a bit. Anyway, I

haven't done this before. I'm not sure where in the Park we'll land.'

'Brilliant!' Flip said. 'It might be in one of the fountains!'

'No, it'll be through another door.' Nick lowered his voice so that none of the others could hear. 'I hope . . .'

They held hands in a ring of four, the stick clutched in Bim's hand, Sorath squawking on Nick's shoulder, the cloud hovering between Flip's ears. They took a deep breath and stepped through the blue crackle of power. And nothing happened.

Bim opened her eyes. 'Hey, we're still here.'

Nick smiled. 'Are we?'

The deck shuddered.

'Did you feel that?' Flip tried to let go of Maxie's hand but their fingers were stuck tight.

The deck shuddered again. Pale figures melted out of the woodwork, running to pull at invisible ropes and speed their ship over the waves. Long-dead sailors raced to their stations, empty eyes fixed and blind to the real world. The two masts stood upright, proudly filling their sails. The ship's captain roared his commands and the ship moved forwards.

'I don't believe it.'

Nick smiled. 'Believe it! I thought we'd sail home. It's the best way to go through a door.'

Out of the jagged entrance of the cave, on to the sea, the old ship creaked and groaned as the wind took her. The deck heaved and the ship sped forwards, away from the black spine of the island and back towards Weston St Brigid. Now they could see what a beautiful ship it had been, red and white painted, masts tall and strong, canvas sails billowing

137

out to trap the wind. Somewhere below were the wrecks of older ships, destroyers, a lone aeroplane and the Tiny Tots Wagontrain. Above them, the sky glowed pale with no clouds, just the blue light of the Door.

Salt spray floated over the rail and Flip grinned. 'Now this is the way to . . .' An electric blue flash and the ship had gone. Flip yelled. 'Oh noooo . . .!'

Squashed into elbows and wet clothes and feet, Flip tried to move. Something clicked under his shoulder and a very small door opened. Too small but, somehow, he fell through it.

The people in the Park gasped as the old clock face sprang open and a whole crowd of bodies fell out. Children in fancy dress, a plump man in an expensive suit and someone whose face was all bony hatred, as big-mouthed as a crocodile . . . They landed in a thrashing heap under the clock tower.

'Must be actors or something,' a man decided. 'Or magicians.' He lifted his camera, ready to get a good shot for his album.

Flip grabbed Qabahl's arm. 'Say "cheese" . . .'

Qabahl shook him off, snarling at the whirr and click of cameras. All around him, camera film bleached to white, but there were too many witnesses . . . Or were there? The crowd surged forwards and Flip yelped, pushed right into Qabahl's stomach. Red, evil eyes burned down at him and the black stick hovered in front of his face.

'Snap like this stick snaps!' Qabahl hissed, and twisted the wood, ready to break it.

Flip twisted . . . His head twisted on his neck, his spine creaked, spinning, bones twisting on bones . . . His cloud tied itself in knots around his pink ears. His shoulders tried to look under his ribs at his

138

nose . . . He saw Qabahl's hands twist harder . . .

Qabahl turned into a frog.

On the small stage, Mrs Weston stared at her grandson. 'Nicholas!' Her knees unlocked and she sat on her chair.

Nick smiled at the gaping crowd. 'I think you'd better all forget that,' he said.

'Er . . . Well . . .' Everyone blinked and shrugged. Already they had forgotten.

One shared blink and the people were laughing again and enjoying the show. It was a great act, really great.

'First class!' the man said, and snapped away with his useless camera and its ruined film. 'Ace magic show!'

Nick turned to Cain. For a moment, Cain could not think of anything to say. He had studied magic all of his life and he still needed his ring to aim his power.

Cain swallowed and managed to speak. 'Well, then. You can do High Magic, Nicholas Weston. But it won't save you.' He straightened his hair and batted dust from his suit. Dust and sand. Several metres away, a frog with sand on its feet croaked and hopped for the shelter of the beach. Cain watched it for a moment and then turned back to look at Nick. He smiled a cold smile. 'Now I'll have to kill you.'

The crowd started to clap as Cain walked away. Startled, he glanced back and a few people shivered. He bowed, and vanished towards St Brigid to wait for his yacht.

Flip bit his lip. Blue sparking, already oozing darkness, the clock-face door waited to be shut. Everyone gazed after Cain, so Flip slid the Key into the blue light.

'Everything that should be in the Other, go back there. Now!'

A whirlwind of dark comets and hairy, scaly, dwarfy objects spun over the gardens. People ducked under flying brownies and gulped as the whole mess shrank down, crunching and squelching into the clock-face.

'Shut!' Flip yelled.

No blue light. No brownies. No Door to the Other. Flip slid the Key back into his pocket and picked his way over the pile of rubbish that the Other Side had left behind . . . Nick's shirt, covered in home-made wine, bits of Mr Sparrow's cake, a dwarf's hat. Nick's lucky stone.

Flip scooped the stone up and handed it to Nick. Stone in pocket, Nick tossed the dwarf's hat from his toe to his hand and spun it. Four pairs of eyes looked towards the clock, then at each other.

'You still want to sell the Key, Flip?' Maxie smiled at him.

'No . . .' Flip grinned at her. 'No, I think I'd better keep it. For a while, anyway.'

Bim glanced at her brother. He wanted to talk to Nick alone. Well, she could take a hint. She jumped backwards, gasped with mock delight and pointed both hands towards the road. 'Oh, Maxie, Maxie! The Pony Club are in the parade. Let's go and pat the ponies!' She caught Nick's knowing grin and stuck her tongue out at him, then grinned back as he pushed the dwarf's hat on to her head. She straightened it, tucked her curls inside and followed Maxie to the ponies.

Flip stirred the heap of cake crumbs with his toe. 'We make quite a team, the four of us. We all worked together. And the stick and everything . . .'

'And me turning Qabahl into a frog? So now you know. I am really weird, Flip.'

Flip looked up. He could never tell what Nick really meant. 'You OK, Nick?'

Nick shrugged. He was still pale but nothing showed on his face. 'It'll take a bit of getting used to. I never thought I could do magic. If I read a spell wrong, anything could happen . . . Yes, I'm OK.' He shook his head. 'They'll be back, you know . . . Cain and Qabahl.'

'I suppose so.'

'We could have got rid of them for good.'

Flip pretended not to hear. 'I wonder what else is in the attic? You know, magic and stuff.'

Nick watched him. 'Well, there's the Sword of Power and Merlin's Spell Book and the Charm Ring and the Magic Mustard . . .'

'You're joking!'

'Am I?'

They looked at each other. Slowly, both of them smiled.

'Come on, Flip. I'm a Weston. It means I get to ride in the big coach in the Opening Parade with Grandma. Want a lift? We can pick Maxie up near the ponies . . .' He pulled a face. 'I'll even let Bim come.'

'Really?'

'Well, Grandma said the Westons and the Sparrows have always been friends. And now I've given you the Friendship Book. She won't mind if you come along. Anyway, suit yourself.'

Flip watched him limp away, leaning on the stick. Sooner or later, Flip decided that he was going to throw Nicholas Weston off Weston Pier. Then the stick's copper head twisted around and winked at him. Flip grinned. 'All right, I'm coming. Hang on, Nick . . .'